In Search of P.E.A.C.E.

A 50-Day Life Transforming Journey

by

Jay Meyer

www.xulonpress.com

Contents

Thank You

To my beautiful wife and children, Lori, Jason, Jordan and Michelle; you gave me something to live for when I was about to give up. Each of you saved and elevated my life in your own unique way.

__Dedication__

This book is dedicated to a couple of people who will never get to read it but they served as catalysts behind it.

Brandon Haskins was a partner at Clay Bridges, a book publisher, and he was working with me during the early stages of this devotional when he was tragically taken from this world. I remember him saying, "Jay I read your blogs, you are a good writer, you should write a book about your life experiences." That was a twenty year old talking to a fifty year old. Brandon was wise beyond his years.

Joe Hitchcock was a childhood friend who tragically left us on April 14, 2009. It was somewhat ironic that the last time I saw Joe alive was when we were serving food to the less fortunate at my church. There are some friends in our lives where our souls become interwoven and this was the case for Joe and me. We played lots of basketball, had lots of laughs, a few fights and shared some tears but most importantly in the last few years leading to Joe's passing, we talked seriously about God.

This book is for you guys. See you in heaven!

How to use this Devotional

Reader beware; this is not a "how to" book. This book has been created in anticipation of giving you a "want to" i.e. a desire to change. Its sole purpose is to provoke thought in your heart, mind and soul and then create a desire to take action.

I've suffered from attention problems since I was a child, and over the years I've had to develop tools to keep me focused. I created my P.E.A.C.E. acronym years ago, and it has helped tremendously with my focus. When I have a God-**Plan**, combined with consistent **Effort**, a positive **Attitude**, a willingness to seek support from and provide support to the **Community** around me, combined with the discipline to take care of my body, mind and spirit in order to have **Energy**; I find my focus to be pretty sharp and my spirit to be at **"P.E.A.C.E."**

The devotional is designed to be completed over a fifty day period and is best done when you have at least thirty minutes to devote to it whether it be first thing in the morning, over lunch or in the evening prior to bedtime.

"In Search of P.E.A.C.E." includes my personal story at the beginning. This was done in order to give you a better understanding about the foundation upon which this devotional was built.

The rubber hits the road when you get to the first cycle of ten sets of personal stories. The stories are stories I have written from the heart (grammatical errors included) over the years for my blog @ www.eagle-launch.com. Connected (very loosely-☺) to each story is one of the five components of the P.E.A.C.E. acronym; (Plan, Effort, Attitude, Community, and Energy). Day one begins with a devotional for Plan, day two-Effort, day three-Attitude, day four-Community, and day five-Energy. In total there will be ten five-day cycles of P.E.A.C.E. devotionals.

At the end of each devotional you will be asked to dive deeper into scripture and reflect and inventory your life through the *Name It, Claim It, and Dump It*, exercise.

There is a "Dump List" at the back of the book and you will add beliefs, thoughts and behaviors to that list as you strive to let go of the old and create a new you.

It takes three to four weeks to create a new habit and another three to four weeks to begin mastering it. In fifty days, you should notice a marked improvement in your faith walk and whatever it is you are trying to overcome, break free from, or improve upon.

. . .and as my mentor Vic always reminded me, there are only two steps in creating a new habit: Start and Continue.

Now get started!

P.E.A.C.E.

Jay

INTRODUCTION

The Story Behind *"In Search of P.E.A.C.E."*

I will never forget the feeling I had during the early morning hours of August 10, 1987. I was beginning what would be my fourth and final withdrawal process from opiates and barbiturates. The nausea, vomiting, diarrhea, and muscle spasms had begun. I had gone "cold turkey" three other times and I was thoroughly frightened going into this fourth attempt to rid myself of drugs forever. After a grueling three-hour intervention by my wife, brother, boss and a guy from AA, I had checked into a chemical dependency center around 10pm the night before. Now it was 2am, and my body started turning inside out.

As I rushed to the bathroom connected to my detox room, I saw something I've never forgotten. Already sitting on the toilet was a man who didn't weigh 100 pounds and could have passed for eighty years old. He had facial hair that seemed to cover his entire face. His skin looked shriveled. In fact, his entire body was shriveled. He raised his head, as he was startled by me opening the door. There were no locks on any of the detox room doors, and I had not been warned that I would be sharing a toilet with a fellow detox patient. The little man raised his head and looked at me and murmured in a faint, weak voice, "What's up, man?"

Luckily, I found another bathroom, as my final cold turkey experience was now beginning. I can remember going back and lying in my bed and thinking of that little, shriveled up man. I later found out my bathroom mate, Willie R., was a "career alcoholic raised on moonshine in the hills of Kentucky." Surprisingly enough, he was only sixty years old. I remember saying to myself; "What's up man? . . .if I only knew."

God brought me into this world in January of 1959, and I've lived my entire life in the small village of Covington, Ohio, located on the west central side of the state. My parents were great role models as they both worked hard and were determined to give my brother and me better lives than they had. My mom was a school teacher, and my dad was a lineman for Dayton Power and Light. They were active participants in my brother's and my lives and still are today. I feel blessed to have been given such great parents, and the best gift they gave me as a human being was an introduction to God at a very early age.

My brother, who was three years older than me, had a quiet disposition, was unassuming and found it much easier to "do as he was told" than to challenge any systems put in place by our parents and/or society.

On the other hand, I was a free spirit and a rebel. I had no regard for boundaries and I always pushed the envelope. I didn't like school because it required me to sit still. Thankfully, I took a liking to basketball, and from the ages of eleven to twenty-three I spent most of my time working on my basketball game and I became a pretty good player. The teams I played on won championships and I received my fair share of individual honors. I even had a couple of offers to play professionally overseas.

Although I didn't like school, I was a good enough student to be accepted into the Ohio Northern University College of Pharmacy upon completion of high school.

Through the years I managed to stay out of trouble for the most part, but had some serious brushes with danger. At the age of sixteen, two weeks after I received my driver's license, I totaled the family's Pinto. I was driving carelessly on a back road and ran head-on into an oak tree. All six of us miraculously walked away from the accident with only bumps and bruises. Yes, six people in a Pinto. . .not a good thing.

I drank my first beer when I was fifteen and it made me feel so good that I proceeded to polish off an entire eight-pack of Genesee Cream Ale. I can remember thinking during this epic moment in my life, "Now I know why people drink!" Alcohol made me feel confident, invincible, and euphoric. Little did I know, I was an alcoholic and a drug addict just waiting to happen.

During my third year at Ohio Northern University I met my wife, Lori Kay Kinnison. As I look back on my college days, Lori was the primary reason why I was able to excel in the classroom as well as on the basketball court. She didn't like to drink or party and out of respect for her, I didn't drink. I still had moments of binge drinking and stupidity.

Life began to speed up in the spring of 1982. I received my pharmacy degree and entered the "real world." Lori and I were married that fall, and our first child, Jason Louis Meyer, entered the world the next summer. Saying that I was a proud daddy would have been an understatement! Of course, I placed a little basketball in his hands the day he was born. I wanted to be the best dad I could be but I was ill-prepared for the responsibilities that came with being a husband and a dad.

Most of my life my goals had been centered around basketball, but now that those days were behind me I had a new dream to focus upon - building wealth. I bought a couple of rental properties and worked three or four pharmacy jobs. The long hours resulted in a need to wind down and I would often drink at night. Lori didn't like it when I drank and asked me to stop and I did.

Shortly thereafter I began taking an "occasional" pill at work to take off the edge and to give me energy. I knew it was wrong, but my need for peace in my head outweighed my desire to not break the law.

Jordan James Meyer was born on February 3, 1986. We named him after the up and coming basketball star, Michael Jordan. At this point in my life I was ingesting drugs, all day, every day. Even though I was high, I can remember Jordan's birth like it happened yesterday. I thanked God for giving me another son as I had always wanted to be the father of two boys. On the way home from the hospital I reached under my car seat and pulled out a bottle of hydrocodone cough syrup, took a swig, and celebrated the birth of my second son.

Within 24 hours after Jordan's birth, he was fighting for his life. He was transported to Children's Medical Center in Dayton, Ohio, where he was put on a ventilator as he was no longer able to breathe on his own. I can remember sitting in the passenger seat of my brother's car following the ambulance down Interstate 75 crying the entire time. The genesis of my tears was due to the fact I thought my son was going to die and I was the cause of his death. You see, I was convinced God was punishing me for the life I was living and he was punishing me by taking something away from me that I so badly wanted.

The next eighteen months of my life were both a blur and quite crazy. We were told Jordan did not have a very good chance of living, and if he did, he would most likely be severely disabled.

Jordan was in the hospital for the better part of the first two months of his life. Lori was consumed with being there for Jordan, and I did what any good addict would do: I used drugs to take away the pain. Over the next eighteen months, my addiction grew to a point where I was taking hits of something every two hours while awake, and consuming anywhere from twenty to thirty pills or "swigs" of cough syrup a day. I reached a point where I would go into withdrawal if I went more than twelve hours without a fix. I needed the drugs to cope with my life, as Jordan was requiring full care from my wife, and every day was a new adventure.

On January 15, 1987, two of my bosses confronted me, as they had figured out my scheme of stealing and consuming drugs. Even though I admitted my problem to them, they had no idea how bad it was. They made me go to counseling and told me if I slipped, it was all over. I wish it would have been that easy.

I tried hard to get it together. I made up my mind to quit for good, but the withdrawal was horrible. I had what seemed like continuous diarrhea and chills, as well as severe depression. I couldn't take it any longer and I started using/stealing a different type of opiate along with an anti-anxiety drug. I was off to the races once again.

Lori and I decided we needed a vacation, so we took a trip to Florida in March of 1987. I figured this would be a good time to get off the drugs, and I decided the only drugs I would take with me would be drugs for diarrhea to help lessen the withdrawal while still being able to function. (Actually, this was the second time I went "cold turkey" in Florida on vacation. The first time had happened two years earlier when no one was aware of my problem. At that time, I told Lori I had a bad case of food poisoning, as I stayed in bed in our hotel room during most of the vacation. I relapsed as soon as we got home.)

I went into withdrawal during the car ride down to Florida, so I began to take the anti-diarrhea medication. Lori thought I had been clean and sober since January 15th and it was now the middle of March. In spite of the anti-diarrhea medication, my intestines were still turning inside out and once again I was bed-ridden during a "vacation" in Florida. Little did I know, a life-changing event was about to take place.

Because of all the drugs I had put into my body over the previous four years, I blew a hole in the duodenal section of my stomach and required emergency surgery to save my life.

The juices in our stomach are quite acidic, and because of the hole I had blown in my stomach, my stomach juices were leaking into my abdominal cavity and the juices were eating away at my organs. Imagine pouring *Drano* or *Liquid Plumber* directly on your organs. . .that was the pain I was experiencing. The pain was so excruciating that I was begging God to take me. I wanted to die, and in a way it would have been a convenient way to "disappear" from the mess I had created in my life. Eventually I went into shock, and I still have trouble recalling the rest of the night, other than what Lori has told me.

It took the doctors almost eight hours to figure out what was wrong with me, and if it wasn't for Lori calling a friend of ours back home, who was a surgeon and a Christian, I would not be alive today. After she explained my symptoms to our surgeon friend, he diagnosed me as having a perforated duodenal ulcer and told those caring for me that I needed emergency surgery.

I was transferred to Warner Robbins Georgia, where emergency surgery was performed and my life was saved. The bad news was that they gave me an order for intravenous Demerol (an opiate) for my pain. Demerol is a powerful opiate and my addiction was off to the races again.

Over the next several months I found myself using different forms of opiates that I had not used in the past, to not be caught by my bosses. I began to get sloppy in my ways and Lori picked up on the fact that I was becoming more and more distant. One day she finally confronted me and told me she had had enough.

I was at a crossroads. There was a part of me that wanted to do the right thing, but I was totally powerless over the drugs. I was now a full-blown drug addict, and that simply meant that my entire life was dependent upon getting my fixes, even if it meant losing those things I loved the most. Addiction is crazy, because as a husband and dad I would take a bullet for my wife and kids any day of the week, but I could not stop taking drugs for them.

On the evening of August 8, 1987, I was sitting alone in the darkness of our family room and I began thinking of how I could take my own life and in turn relieve my pain once and for all. I had started suffering from paranoia coupled with depression, and had become nothing more than a shell of the person I once was.

Thank God, my thoughts of ending it all were somehow replaced with thoughts of Lori and my kids having to go through life without me. At that time Jason was four, Jordan was one-and-a-half and we were pregnant with our third child, Michelle. I was so distraught, I wanted to die, but the values of responsibility my parents had instilled in me most likely saved my life. In a moment of "weakness," I raised my hands up in the air and said, "God, help me, I don't care how you do it, but help me!" Up until this point during my "drug years," I had turned my back on God.

The next day was a Sunday. When I walked through the front door of our house after a long day of work (I was working almost every day because of my need to be around my drugs and my desire to have wealth), sitting in the living room of our house was my wife, brother, one of my bosses, and a recovering alcoholic and drug addict named Rusty.

They were there to tell me it was over. It is important to remember my prayer from the night before; God had answered my prayer. It is also important to understand the sickness of addiction, because I told them to all go to hell and that I would fix my problem on my own and it was they who had a problem.

Thank God, Rusty was there. Rusty had been right where I was about five years earlier. He kept asking questions that made me realize how sick I really was. I was so out of touch with reality and in denial and this intervention helped open my eyes to reality. Finally, after three hours, they broke me and I agreed to go to treatment. On August 9, 1987 around 9pm, I walked through the doors of the emergency room at Greene Memorial Hospital and an hour later I was officially a resident of Greene Hall Treatment Center, located in Xenia, Ohio.

My life was about to change forever. The four people in that intervention saved my life—but it didn't happen overnight.

It took a couple of weeks to get through the physical aspects of withdrawal and about three years to learn how to cope with the mental aspects of a "brain no longer on drugs." Yes, three years.

Treatment introduced me to a whole new world. I learned addiction is a disease that takes away our ability to think and act rationally. I was introduced to many tools that I would need to utilize a day at a time to have a chance at whipping it. I can remember the treatment director speaking with the group I was with. There were thirty-two of us, and he said, "Look around this room, because statistics tell us only two of you are going to make it and stay clean from this point forward."

I now had a new dream to stay sober. . .I knew my life and family depended on it.

During the first few weeks of recovery, I really struggled with the fact that I would never be able to drink and/or drug again. I was taught about the progressive nature of the disease. Even though we stop using or drinking or acting out, the disease keeps progressing and when we take a drink or a pill or act out again, it is a matter of time until we are worse than we were before. I had witnessed that in my two or three futile attempts to quit.

Early on, I can remember thinking it would be impossible for me to not drink and/or drug, and then I started wondering if I really had a problem or if I could get my life in order and go back to at least drinking again.

At the end of my second week at the treatment center, I received word from home that the State Pharmacy Board, the County Sheriff's Department and the DEA had all been contacted by one of the pharmacists I was working for. When I found this out, I went into an immediate mental tailspin as the consequences of my decisions were beginning to come to pass.

Not too long after that, an agent from the DEA came to the treatment center to speak with me. I was never so nervous in all of my life than when I met with that man. I decided I had nothing to lose by being honest with him, as I figured I was going to jail and would never practice pharmacy again. I remember getting quite emotional as I told this man my story and I kept telling him I was not a bad person and didn't want to steal, but my addiction had forced me to do it. He informed me that I was obviously facing major felony charges for drug theft. He was also trying to figure out whether or not I was selling the drugs because there were so many missing. I didn't sell, I consumed, and I had consumed well over 25,000 doses over a five-year period. Something I am not proud of, but something you need to know to understand the seriousness of my situation and the insanity associated with the disease of addiction.

Needless to say, after my talk with the DEA agent, I was devastated and as low as I had ever been. It almost felt like paralysis had taken over my body, mind and soul. I felt like a giant lump was in my stomach. I was at a point where I felt absolutely powerless. In that moment, I could finally see what I had done and where I was. I wanted to change.

I didn't know it then, but in my mind and spirit I had taken the first step in the Twelve Step process, *"Admitted*

I am powerless over drugs and alcohol and my life had become unmanageable."

Later that night, I was totally out of solutions and desperate for a cure. I was twenty-eight years old and had totally screwed up everything. I had received a letter from a Christian friend that day, and in her letter she encouraged me to be "born again" and accept Jesus as Lord and savior. I was desperate, and even though I had no clue what accepting Jesus meant, I said a prayer and did it. I told Him He could have all of me for the rest of my life, regardless of whether I went to jail or ever practiced pharmacy again. I simply wanted a shot at saving my family, my reputation, and making something good come out of this horrible situation I had created from my own decisions.

Unbeknownst to me at the time, I had just done steps two and three. *"Came to believe a power greater than me could restore my sanity (2), and turned my will and my life over to the care of God (3)."*

On September 8, 1987, I was discharged from inpatient treatment. Little did I know, those days I spent in the Greene Hall Chemical Dependency Unit were about to jump start an unbelievable life journey.

Since August 9, 1987, with the help of God, I've been able to not only rebuild my life, but do things I never would have dreamed of doing, all because I've remained clean and sober, and drew closer to God, one day at a time.

It's taken tons of work, lots of prayer, and many great mentors, as well as a loving family. Staying sober was a bitch in the beginning, and I worked harder at that than anything I had ever done in my life. Because of my pending court case and pharmacy license situation, I could not work for over a year after I got out of treatment, and even then I could only work part-time. This in turn created financial difficulties for my family. The dream of becoming a millionaire turned into a desire to simply stay out of bankruptcy.

Slowly but surely, things started changing as the curses of my past began to be replaced by blessings. The first "huge" sober blessing was the birth of my third child, Michelle.

After the difficulties Jordan endured, it was only normal for me to be worried that the same thing would happen with Michelle. Michelle Marie Meyer was born healthy, on January 15, 1988, just a little over five months after I got sober, but more importantly on Lori's birthday and exactly one year from the date I was first confronted by my bosses!

Another huge boost to my morale took place between my second and third year of sobriety, as the DEA decided to not file any charges against me and I was able to keep my pharmacy license and go back to work full-time. Do you believe in miracles?

I must say, I never walked a straighter line in all of my life than I did once I got out of treatment. I would send weekly reports of my treatment plan efforts and alcoholics anonymous (AA) meeting attendance to the DEA agent and the State Board of Pharmacy. They knew I was serious about getting well. My sponsor, Vic A., played a huge part in relieving my fears during this thirty-month process of waiting. He kept saying, "Jay, God is the ultimate judge and he will determine whether or not you will go to jail and lose your pharmacy license. You just need to keep doing the next right thing."

Lori stayed by my side, and my family members on both sides of the family were my biggest supporters as I embarked on this recovery journey, one day at a time.

By the grace of God, we were able to raise a loving, God-fearing family where our oldest (Jason) and youngest (Michelle) were blessed by gaining their college degrees from Dartmouth College, an Ivy League school. I humbly present this information only because never in my wildest dreams did I think I would be able to produce such well-rounded, intelligent kids. Both of them gained admission to Dartmouth because of their prowess on the basketball court, as each of them were All-State performers in high school and they both became captains on their college basketball teams. God is good!

Our middle child, Jordan, whom we named after Michael Jordan, ended up being my Jordan River, as it was he who helped me cross over to the "promised land." As I look back on that pivotal night in August of 1987, when I so badly wanted to die, I can remember looking at a picture of my two boys, thinking I could not abandon them, especially Jordan with all of his difficulties. Unable to talk yet full of the Holy Spirit, as indicated through his sparkling blue eyes, Jordan has served as a great stabilizing force for our entire family. We never take things for granted, nor do we ever take things too seriously. Jordan helps us keep things in perspective.

After years of working on the resentment I held against the pharmacist who "threw me under the bus" by reporting my drug problem to the DEA and the State Pharmacy Board, I finally came to grips with the fact it was my actions and poor decisions that caused him to do what he did. In 2007, I was able to reconcile with this man and make amends to him as I took full responsibility for what had happened. It never ceases to amaze me how transforming God's power can be in our lives.

The pharmacy boss who was involved in my intervention, and from whom I stole thousands of dollars' worth of drugs, forgave me and asked me to come back to work for him, and ended up making me a partner in his pharmacy business. We built the business into a highly respected Ohio nursing home pharmacy and sold in 1998. We were both blessed financially through this venture.

After the sale, I continued as president of this business, and along with the help of my new owners/partners, we were able to grow it almost ten-fold over a nine-year period and became a well-known entity in the United States.

In the spring of 2010, I retired from the pharmacy world and now spend my time helping others through coaching and public speaking.

So what is the reason for this book?

There were many reasons why I not only got sober, but was able to stay sober and learn how to live life on life's terms. Back when I was in the chemical dependency center we were required to do a morning recovery program that involved reading a devotional and spending time with God in prayer and reflection. I did this every day while I was in treatment, and have done this every day since. It is the one thing I have never stopped doing, and have come to realize this morning ritual is the foundation of my life today.

Spending time with God to start my day is the most important thing I do every day. It is my way of surrendering everything I have to God, and in turn being free from the stressors of the world and placing focus on enhancing my life with God's help, to be a blessing for others. This time I spend with God improves my ability to be the best husband, dad, son, brother, leader, and friend I can be. It is that simple.

In the "50-Day Journey," I've taken many years of experience as a user and abuser, and then as a sober person, and combined those experiences into real-life reflections tied to scripture that I hope will have meaning to you and assist you in your quest of becoming everything God wants you to be. Although we may think there are limits to our abilities and possibilities; God proves there are none. . .I write from experience.

Isaiah 40:31 (NIV), ". . .but those who hope in the Lord will renew their strength. They will soar on wings like eagles; they will run and not grow weary, they will walk and not be faint."

P.E.A.C.E.

CYCLE ONE OF TEN

A grateful heart without "want" is a heart God "wants" and will be filled plentifully with what God knows it needs.

Plan

1-The Power to Continue

Psalm 91:14-16 (NIV), "Because he loves me," says the Lord, "I will rescue him; I will protect him, for he acknowledges my name. He will call upon me, and I will answer him; I will be with him in trouble, I will deliver him and honor him. With long life will I satisfy him and show him my salvation."

A few years ago, I had just completed my first marathon. I had achieved my goal of breaking four hours, and although I was completely wasted physically,

I was feeling pretty good about my accomplishment. The first thing I did after the race was place a large "chaw" of tobacco in my mouth. . .I was celebrating my accomplishment. (I started chewing tobacco when I was eighteen years old, and twenty-five years later, I was still chewing.)

As I slowly crept/crawled up the street to my car, I was congratulating other marathoners etc. . . with this big chaw of tobacco in my cheek. Then suddenly a thought crossed my mind *(most effective thoughts come from God)*. It was something like this. . ."how crazy is this, I just completed one of the most physical athletic tests known to man and I am celebrating by putting 'dung' in my mouth and body and in turn taking years from my life!?"

I remember how awkward I felt in that moment and decided it was time to quit. . .for good. Quitting was not the problem, as I had "quit" hundreds of times in the past. . .staying quit was another issue. My AA sponsor always reminded me there were two steps in breaking a bad habit and/or creating a new habit: *start and continue*. Most of us have no problem starting, but it is the continue part that becomes quite difficult, if not impossible for many of us.

I got up the next morning and was already craving tobacco to go along with my coffee. But this time instead of giving in to the craving, I had a little talk with God and said, "This sucks, I want to stay quit but I can't, please give me one good reason to stay quit." Then I heard God's voice (I've only heard God's voice a couple of times in my life). . .He said, "Because you love Me." I was like, "Wait, God, what does that mean?" Check out Psalm 91 above.

Then I sat and reflected and figured out what God was saying to me. It was something like this: "Jay, you say you love Me, and you know your body is My temple, therefore you will stay quit simply because. . .you love Me." (An inference directly from God about being a hypocrite is a great way to get one's attention.)

As I've mentioned before, a goal will not be achieved without a plan. My plan for achieving my new goal of staying quit from tobacco was plain and simple. . .I was going to seek God's help early and often, every day. . .just like I had to do and still do with my drug and alcohol addiction.

From that point forward I placed, my goal of staying quit in God's hands one day at a time, and eventually the cravings disappeared as well as the desire to ever use again. IT WAS NOT EASY, BUT NOTHING WORTH-WHILE IN LIFE IS EVER EASY! Staying quit certainly worked more effectively when I involved God.

Diving Deeper:

Additional Scripture: Mark 11:24, Jeremiah 29:11, Proverbs 16:3

Name IT: Do you battle with sustaining positive change in your life?

Claim IT: What would you like to change?

Dump IT: Add whatever is standing in your way of positive change to your Dump List and prayerfully turn it over to God one day at a time.

Effort

1-Distractions

Proverbs 14:23 (NIV), "All hard work brings a profit, but mere talk leads only to poverty."

The famous football coach and now TV analyst and motivational speaker, Lou Holtz, once said: "When it's all said and done, there is more said than done."

There are two steps in achieving a goal. . .*start and continue,* and the step all of us struggle with the most is *continue.*

We all know that any type of success in life takes hard work and **Effort**, and if you are reading this devotion, you are probably a person who is trying to better yourself by whipping an addiction and/or creating a new healthy habit.

The longer I live, the more I realize that it's not just the effort in our work ethic that determines the fruits of our labor, but it is the quality of our effort. Quality effort requires the discipline to stay on task day after day, and this takes the ability to avoid distractions.

One of the biggest distractions that often impede our effort in continuing and accomplishing our goals is talk. I used to own a fitness center, and the people who accomplished their fitness goals were the ones who came in and did their workout with very little conversation. They stayed on task, and if they talked they were motivating their workout partner to go the extra mile. Let's face it, talk is cheap.

The major difference between productive people and organizations, and unproductive people and organizations, is how much or how little they talk. . .about nonsense. . .about things. I've witnessed organizations having meetings prior to meetings and after meetings to do. . .I don't know what?! I know people who take ten minutes to explain a one-sentence circumstance.

It is obviously much easier to talk than it is to do.

One of my favorite quotes of all time comes from the late Eleanor Roosevelt; "small minds and people talk about people, average minds and people talk about things, great minds and people talk about ideas."

Where are you today? Do you spend most of your time talking about "things" and other people? We all know talk is cheap and comforting, but we also need to remember and believe what Solomon says about talk in Proverbs 14:23, wasteful talk impedes our ability to profit and will eventually lead to poverty of the mind, body, and soul. Wasteful talk impedes our ability to put forth a quality effort.

Challenge yourself to limit your complaints as well as your talk about things and other people, and concentrate on conversing about ways to better yourself and the world. Productive effort results in the continuation of the achievement of your goals.

Diving Deeper:

Additional Scripture: Ecclesiastes 5:1-7, James 3:6, Proverbs 10:19, Proverbs 17:28, Proverbs 29:20

Name IT: Do you talk more than you "walk?"

Claim IT: If yes, why?

Dump IT: Add the "why" from above to your
             Dump List and prayerfully turn it over
             to God one day at a time.

Attitude

1-Take Control of Your "Space"and Take Control of Your Attitude

2 Corinthians 3:17-18 (NIV) "Now the Lord is the Spirit, and where the Spirit of the Lord is, there is freedom. And we, who with unveiled faces all reflect the Lord's glory, are being transformed into his likeness with ever-increasing glory, which comes from the Lord, who is the Spirit."

One of my favorite sayings to my kids has always been, "You've got to control what you can control and your attitude is one thing you have control over." A for

Attitude is strategically located right smack dab in the middle of the P.E.A.C.E acronym. Attitude affects the outcome of almost everything we do.

There are an abundance of studies showing that people with positive attitudes are healthier, live longer, and are more effective on the job. Years ago, when clinging to his life in a German concentration camp, Victor Frankl found a way to survive the mental anguish he experienced as he witnessed those around him being killed and tortured during the Holocaust. He was quoted as saying, "Everything can be taken from a man or a woman but one thing. The last of human freedoms to choose one's attitude in any given set of circumstances to choose one's own way."

Later Frankl was quoted as saying: "Between stimulus and response there is a space. In that space is our power to choose our response. In our response lies our growth and freedom." Stephen Covey, the author of one the greatest self-help books of all time, "The 7 Habits of Highly Effective People" used this Frankl thought to help people understand they have control over their attitude and ultimately their lives, and the control lies in the space between stimulus and response.

Think about it: we are stimulated all day long and we respond to the stimulus. How many times do we let other people, places, and things control our responses and ultimately our attitude, and we think nothing of it?

Back when I was in the pits of my addiction, the drugs and alcohol had control over my "space." Co-dependent people allow other people to control their "space." People who hate their jobs are usually allowing their "space" to be controlled by a boss or a co-worker. Some people allow the weather to control their "space." Depressed people allow depression to control their "space". . .I could go on and on.

Take back your "space" between **stimulus and response.** Those people with the most effective attitudes are people who have learned to control the space between stimulus and response. There are many different ways to regain control of your "space" and here are a few that have worked for me.

1. Having a plan for your life is the first step in taking ownership of the space between stimulus and response. If I know where I'm going, it is hard for other people, places, and things to invade that "space" and corrupt my attitude.

2. Have daily prayer time and Bible reading; especially read the gospels. Learning how Jesus responded to situations is a great way to learn how to handle situations you will face throughout the day. The book of Proverbs also serves as a great guide for living life effectively.

3. Try hard to maintain a conscious contact with God throughout the day. When you do, suddenly God begins to control your "space."

4. Treat your body right by nurturing it with good things. When I say good things, I mean music, literature, food, rest, etc... You will be amazed at how this will strengthen your "space" and positively impact your response.

5. Until you are able to stand on your own two feet and keep other people, places, and things out of your "space," create boundaries and stay away from those

things that historically have controlled your "space" and ultimately your attitude.

6. Surround yourself with people who control their "space" and subsequently have the positive attitude you are seeking.

With all of this being said, the bottom line is this; as Christians, the "space" between stimulus and response should be filled with the Holy Spirit. God gives us the ability to respond as Jesus would in any situation. God knows we will never be perfect at this, but I believe he wants to see us reach and grow towards having our "space" filled with the Holy Spirit.

As Frankl said, "In our response lies our growth and freedom." Once we begin to control our "space" by allowing God's spirit to flow through us, we will experience unbelievable growth and freedom in our attitude. And remember. . .this is all a process, it is not an event. Try to get better one day at a time.

Diving Deeper:

Additional Scripture: John 15:26-27, Colossians 3:15, Philippians 4:6-7

Name IT: What is your "space" looking like these days? Is it clean so the Holy Spirit can effectively guide you?

Claim IT: If not, what people, places, and/or things are controlling/corrupting your "space"?

Dump IT: Add whatever is corrupting your "space" to your Dump List and prayerfully turn it over to God one day at a time.

Community

1-Community. . .receiving and giving

Proverbs 13:20 (NIV), "He who walks with the wise grows wise, but a companion of fools suffers harm."

As I've mentioned previously, great people not only put forth positive **effort**, with a can-do **attitude**, and take care of their bodies to have **energy**, while executing their life **plan**, but they understand nothing great happens without effective interaction with the **community** around them.

Anything I've been successful at in my life has involved great support and help from other people in the community around me. In turn, my continued success in these various aspects of my life has involved me supporting and helping other people.

I got sober and stayed sober through the help of many people. I learned the best way for me to stay sober was to help others stay sober. I became a pretty good basketball player because of the coaches who taught me and the players I trained with, and then I spent a significant amount of my life helping others with their basketball. I built my business career through the help and support of many people; today I help others build their businesses. I learned to train for and compete in triathlons from the help and support of other people; today I help others train for and compete in endurance sports.

I remember waking to a text message years ago that went like this: "Jay, when you get up, please call me, it is an emergency." This was a person I was helping with his addiction problem. I gave him a call and we talked. In a nutshell, this person was becoming "foolish" and wanted to stop the behavior. Instead of calling another active fool or acting out on his own by listening to "the committee in his head," he contacted a recovering "fool turned wise" for help. This person ended up turning away from his foolishness and got back on the road to recovery, all because he turned to wisdom and away from his own foolishness.

It's our choice who we walk with. Today I tell people to walk with the winners, and the winners are people who not only are following God, but have a positive **attitude,** combined with **energy** and a focused **effort** in executing a **plan,** and also people who are helpful and help-able in the **community** around them.

There is a great saying in the recovery **community:** "You can't keep what you've received from others unless you give it away."

<u>Diving Deeper:</u>

Additional Scripture-Hebrews 10:24-25, Acts 2:42-47, Galatians 6:2, Romans 12:3-13

Name IT: Are you walking with winners today?

Claim IT: If not, who will you try to walk with?

Dump IT: Add all thoughts and beliefs causing you to go back to "old faces" to your Dump List and prayerfully turn them over to God one day at a time.

Energy

1-Energy and God's temple

1 Corinthians 6:19 (NIV), "Do you not know that your body is a temple of the Holy Spirit, who is in you, whom you have received from God?"

As I've mentioned before, there are five key components in the way I live my life that enhance my ability to stay sober and live effectively one day at a time. I use the acronym P.E.A.C.E to keep it simple for me. The five ingredients include **P**lanning, **E**ffort, **A**ttitude, **C**ommunity, and **E**nergy. I ask for the Holy Spirit to fuel these components each and every day, and for the most part my days are productive.

The other day I was at the gas station, fueling up, when a friend approached me and said, "Jay, what can I do to get more energy?" I said, "Get some rest, exercise routinely, eat the right foods and pray to God for energy." She looked at me and laughed and said, "I don't have time to do all of that." I told her, "I don't have time to NOT do all that."

Without Energy, we can kiss "goodbye" any chances of effectively working the first four letters of the P.E.A.C.E. acronym effectively.

Without **Energy**, it is difficult to put forth maximum **Effort** in accomplishing our **Plans**. Without Energy, it is virtually impossible to maintain a positive **Attitude** to accomplish our Plans. Without Energy, it becomes extremely difficult to work with others in the **Community** around us to accomplish our Plans. Energy is the keystone to effective living, and effective living means we are doing the right thing for God in all of the roles we are involved in.

If you are feeling run down and unable to accomplish your plans, take a look at how much time you are devoting to supplying your body with what it needs to have energy.

Are you sleeping at least 6-8 hours a night? One thing that helps me is that I try to get fifty hours of sleep each week, and I often find myself using the weekend to "catch up" to that goal.

Is your diet well rounded? Do you eat a healthy breakfast? Are you staying away from fats and sugars (this is the tough one for me)?

Are you exercising at least three times a week for thirty minutes?

But most importantly, are you including these vital objectives on your **weekly Plan**?

If you struggle with doing any of the above. . .try writing them down as a part of your plan. If you feel the best when you get eight hours of sleep, then make a plan for how you are going to accomplish it. If you struggle with staying disciplined with your diet, then write out your eating plans every week. If you have trouble sticking with a routine exercise program, make a plan for how you will get it accomplished on a weekly basis.

You will be amazed at how you suddenly find time to get these things done once you include them in your weekly plan. Then you will be amazed at how much more you will get done every week because you have energy. I only write from personal experience.

One last thing. . .you may want to read Paul's words in 1 Corinthians above the first thing every morning. Our body is God's temple. Are you treating it that way?

Diving Deeper:

Additional Scripture: 1 Corinthians 6:20, 1 Corinthians 3:16-17, Romans 12:1

Name IT: Do you have energy the majority of the time?

Claim IT: If not, what is preventing you from having energy?

Dump IT: Note on your Dump List the one thing that is preventing you from having energy and prayerfully turn it over to God one day at a time.

P.E.A.C.E.

CYCLE TWO OF TEN

~

Man cannot expand what he has until he is willing to give it away.

Plan

2-"Fixing" our gaze. . .

Proverbs 4:25 (NIV), "Let your eyes look straight ahead, fix your gaze directly before you."

*Y*ears ago, when I returned home from my five-week stay in a chemical dependency center, I hooked up with my first sponsor. I remember this like it was yesterday because what he did that day, though it seemed small at the time, was about to change the course of my life forever.

I remember him asking me if I had a daily "planner system" that I worked off of. Of course my response was, "No, I've got a great memory and do not need a planner." He then said if I wanted him to be my sponsor, I had to listen to him and he required his sponsorees to plan their weeks every Sunday and review them with him every Sunday evening.

So I decided to listen, and slowly but surely I began to plan my weeks. Back then, my plans were centered on my recovery as I went to AA meetings daily as well as intense outpatient counseling. Slowly but surely my plans started involving other responsibilities such as my family and job and then they eventually evolved into my current plans which are focused on my faith walk, my health, my family, my business, my profession, and the recovery community.

I often chuckle when people comment on how disciplined I am, because at my core I am as unfocused as anyone I know, but having a plan helps to keep my gaze "fixed" and my eyes focused straight ahead.

As I look back, planning was very difficult for me. I was a person who did not want to miss a thing and thus always liked to keep my schedule "open," while on the other hand it took effort to plan, and unless I liked what I was planning for, I didn't plan for it.

This type of behavior was just another symptom of my challenges with my attention disorder, but even more it is a symptom many of us in recovery experience; and that is a general lack of discipline.

Lack of discipline manifests itself in two very distinct yet opposite ways. Either a person is involved in way too many activities, or they are not involved in anything. The first behavior creates a "manic" state of mind, and the other creates a "depressed" state of mind.

So, what is the best way to get disciplined and avoid the emotional roller coaster ride a non-disciplined life creates? It is pretty simple, though often painful in the beginning. . .create a PLAN!

Planning weekly and reviewing your plans daily for follow-thru and adjustments, is the best way to achieve balance and be productive in a very unbalanced world.

There is an amazing power that we receive whenever we write something down. For me, it allows me to "fix my gaze directly before me" instead of all around me, and it also allows me to get some amazing things done in the 168 hours God gives us each week.

If you find yourself distracted and not focused, or possibly sitting on the "pity pot," with nothing to do. . .try "fixing" your gaze by developing a plan. I guarantee your life will become more disciplined than you ever could have imagined.

And, oh yeah, **"Commit to the Lord whatever you do, and your plans will succeed." (Proverbs 16:3 NIV)**

Diving Deeper:

Additional Scripture: Proverbs 16:9, Proverbs 21:5

Name IT: Do you have a planning system in place?

Claim IT: If not, what is preventing you from performing this important action?

Dump IT: Note on your Dump List the one thing
              that is preventing you from creating a
              plan for your life and prayerfully turn it
              over to God one day at a time.

Effort

2- Listening is Effort

**Proverbs 1:33 (NIV), "But all who listen to me will
live in safety, and be at ease, without fear of harm."**

For years I have had to learn how to handle my very
"active" mind. Basically, I am a self-diagnosed sufferer
of Attention Deficit/Hyperactivity Disorder (ADHD),
and I've learned to live with the disorder pretty effectively. Having a plan with goals, rest, exercise, healthy
eating habits, vitamin supplements, and a trust in and a
life driven by a power greater than myself (God/Jesus)
has worked wonders in allowing me to function at a
pretty high level even though my mind is constantly
trying to "race." A common defect for those of us with

ADHD is the inability to listen. This has gotten me into a lot of trouble over the years, but slowly but surely I am getting there. . .unless you ask my wife.

A common defect in Jesus' followers is what I refer to as Spiritual ADHD. We profess to know the Word, yet live a life that demonstrates otherwise.

In Proverbs, God says if we listen to Him we will live in peace, untroubled by fear of harm. The key here is to listen, and listening takes action. Listening means hearing attentively, listening means trying to understand what someone else is telling you to the point you can explain it back to them. Do you ever wonder if God is watching us after we read scripture to see if we really are "listening" to His Word?

Spiritual ADHD for God-loving people presents itself in various ways, but there are usually two symptoms that are more profound than the rest. The first presents itself as a life in turmoil and not at peace. This life is often lived in fear of "something." The other symptom is a life of self-righteousness, where Christians "preach" and "teach" the word much more effectively than they live it.

Let's be honest, we all have our moments when Spiritual ADHD takes over. The key is to keep these episodes in "moments" and not allow them to turn into days, weeks, months, and years.

The best way to keep Spiritual ADHD in check is to not only spend time in the Word, but to try your best to live the Word. Having time set aside in the morning to read scripture and then pray and envision how it will apply to your life is a great way to start the day. During this time, it is also important to list your fears and turn them over to God. Remember, fear is from the evil one, and God beats evil every time. Plugging into account-ability groups and interacting with healthy account-ability people will also help in keeping Spiritual ADHD in check.

Last but not least, try hard to let your actions speak louder than your words. . .especially when "nobody" is watching you. It takes effort but it is well worth it.

Diving Deeper:

Additional Scripture: James 1:19, Mark 4:24, Psalm 46:10

Name IT: Is my life a "reflection" of a life that listens to God?

Claim IT: What prevents me from being a good listener?

Dump IT: Note on your Dump List the one thing that is preventing you from being a good listener and prayerfully turn it over to God one day at a time.

Attitude

2-Resentments and Attitude-Choosing God Over the World

James 4:1-10 (NIV), "What causes fights and quarrels among you? Don't they come from your desires

that battle within you? You want something but don't get it. You kill and covet, but you cannot have what you want. You quarrel and fight. You do not have, because you do not ask God. When you ask, you do not receive, because you ask with wrong motives, that you may spend what you get on your pleasures. You adulterous people, don't you know that friendship with the world is hatred toward God? Anyone who chooses to be a friend of the world, becomes an enemy of God. Or do you think Scripture says without reason that the spirit he caused to live in us envies intensely? But he gives us more grace. That is why Scripture says: *God opposes the proud but gives grace to the humble.* Submit yourselves, then, to God. Resist the devil, and he will flee from you. Come near to God and he will come near to you. Wash your hands, you sinners, and purify your hearts, you double-minded. Grieve, mourn and wail. Change your laughter to mourning and your joy to gloom. Humble yourselves before the Lord, and he will lift you up."

The other night I was at a Twelve Step Meeting and the topic was resentment. Most people in recovery know that one of the primary reasons we drink, drug, or act out is because of resentments. Some people drink their entire life because of something that happened to them when they were five years old. There are "normal" people who carry resentments for a lifetime also and they don't drink, but you can usually tell who they are because they are angry and miserable and always find a way to blame others for their lot in life.

Resentments are from the devil, and as long as we give in to them and continue to carry them, bad things will happen and the devil will be happy.

When you look at the scripture from James above, the second verse (third sentence) kind of hits the nail on the head. We want something and don't get it or we get something we don't want. Wanting what others have, or wanting more or less than what we already have and/ or comparing ourselves to others is a sure fire way for jealousy and resentment to creep in, and it usually manifests itself through an angry spirit where we "quarrel and fight" with the world and/or between our ears. This is suicide for an alcoholic or addict, and plain misery for the "normal" person.

James tells us that the genesis of anger and resentment is our "friendship with the world." He also tells us, "You do not have because you do not ask God." What he is saying is that we are seeking our happiness from the world instead of God, and that is a no-win proposition.

At the end of these verses from James, he gives us a solution and it is pretty simple;

1. "Submit yourself to God" (not the world).
2. "Resist the devil and he will flee from you" (tell the devil to take a hike. . .I often use stronger words than that)
3. "Come near to God and he will come near to you" (let go of the world and grab onto God).
4. "Wash your hands, you sinners and purify your hearts you double-minded" (repent your shortcomings to God).
5. "Grieve, mourn and wail. Change your laughter to mourning and joy to gloom" (turn ALL your anger over to God).

6. "Humble yourselves before the Lord and he will lift you up" (by doing the five steps above, we put ourselves in a mental and spiritual state (i.e., humble/humility) where God can work with us and lift us up no matter what the circumstance).

If you want to be relatively happy, joyous, and free the majority of the time, do the above steps on a daily basis (these are steps ten and eleven from the Christian Twelve Steps). You will slowly find yourself being lifted up and above your worldly tendencies.

<u>Diving Deeper:</u>

Additional Scripture: Proverbs 20:22, Matthew 5:38-48

Name IT: What resentments and/or jealousies are you holding onto?

Claim IT: Are you ready to release them?

Dump IT: Note your number one resentment on your Dump List and prayerfully turn it over to God one day at a time.

Community

2-Who's in your "community-space"?

Hebrews 10:24-25 (NIV), *"And let us consider how we may spur one another on toward love and good deeds. Let us not give up meeting together, as some are in the habit of doing, but let us encourage one another. . ."*

On more than one occasion, I've been asked to deliver a message to the third-year pharmacy students at the annual Ohio Northern University pharmacy mentorship dinner. The third year is a pivotal year in the life of a pharmacy student. It's a time for these soon-to-be professionals to begin thinking about the real world and what they want to do in three years after they graduate as Doctors of Pharmacy. The mentorship program is an opportunity to bring back pharmacy "veterans" like myself to lend guidance to these future health care professionals. I have to pinch myself when considering my past. . .to think I am asked to mentor pharmacy students???? *If this isn't evidence of how Jesus can turn a life around, then I don't know what is.*

The point I make to the third-year pharmacy students is very basic, yet paramount to their future success, and of course something I can totally relate to. I share with them that "they will become the decisions they make in their life," and that the people they choose to seek guidance from, i.e. their mentors, will play a big part in their decision-making process and subsequent successes and/ or failures. It is pretty easy for me to compare and contrast my crash and burn mentors from the past with my uplifting mentors of today.

Years ago Capital One commercials used the tag line, "What's in your wallet?" Their whole goal is to convince consumers the Capital One credit card is the best. I have to wonder if that might be an oxymoron (best credit card??). Take a moment and ask yourself, "Who's in your space, i.e., community?" Who are your mentors? Today I try my best to seek guidance from others who will enhance my behavior, and in turn better my life. I try to keep my "space/community" as crisp and focused as possible, and it begins with having Jesus at the center and strong Jesus followers close by. In my previous life, I sought guidance from those who would help me **justify** my behavior.

Ask yourself who you've sought guidance from recently. Is it someone who simply justified your decision, or is it someone who challenged it and ultimately enhanced it?

By the way, not seeking guidance qualifies as finding "someone" to justify your behavior. . .can you say "the committee in your head?" The "committee" was my mentor for the last six months of my drug life. . .there is no worse place to be.

If you want to be excellent seek excellence from excellent others. If you want to be average, seek average from average others. If you want to be nothing, seek no guidance.

Fill your space with people who will encourage your growth by helping you make the right decisions. You cannot do it alone.

Solomon (the son of King David) tells us in Proverbs 11:14, *"there is safety in having many advisers."*

Make a decision today to fill your "community-space" with great people.

Diving Deeper:

Additional Scripture: Proverbs 27:17, Proverbs 13:20

Name IT: Who are your mentors? Who's helping you with your decisions?

Claim IT: Do you need to enhance your mentors? Are there some people you need to stay away from? Staying away from them does not mean we quit loving them, it simple means we value our growth more than we do having a relationship with them.

Dump IT: Add these people to your Dump List and pray for them to find the same peace and happiness you are in search of today.

Energy

2- Break free from your SHELTER. . .

2 Timothy 1:7 (NIV), "For God did not give us a spirit of timidity, but a spirit of power, of love and of self-discipline."

A few years ago, I recall my wife looking out the back window of our home observing our new "rescue dog," Boyd, sprinting across the yard having fun with his "brother," Onyx. My wife commented, "Five months ago that dog could barely walk." Yes, when we rescued Boyd from the animal shelter, he was fat, lazy, and very un-ambitious.

A couple of days after Boyd left the animal shelter and came to his new home, I took him for a walk. We got about 200 yards into the walk and he sat down and would not go any farther because he was exhausted.

In a matter of weeks, after a good night's sleep, Boyd was up before dawn, hunting animals in our woods with our other dog, Onyx. In the process, he shed twenty-five pounds and found a new freedom, happiness, and energy he hadn't experienced in a long time.

Over the years, I've had the opportunity to help many people in their struggles with addiction, co-dependency, or other obstacles in life. Those who overcome their obstacles find a way to break free from their past and their bad habits, and those who remain in bondage remain slaves to their past, or like my dog prior to his rescue, they continue to live in their self-made "shelters" of isolation.

Unlike my dog Boyd, as human beings, we have the ability to choose whether or not we stay stuck in our old way of living. But, like my dog Boyd, once we break free from the past we find ourselves doing things we never dreamed of doing.

In Timothy, we are told *a spirit of timidity and/or fear is not of God*. God gives us the *spirit of power, love, and self-discipline*. What's interesting is that those three traits are what I see in Boyd today, and it was simply because we "rescued" him from his past life and future fate as an animal shelter dog.

If you are stuck in a rut and low on energy and find yourself thinking the same old thoughts and acting out the same old actions and feeling the same old way, it is time to allow God to "rescue" you from your past and your "shelter." God sent his son to die for all of our sins and to give us His Spirit of power, love and self-discipline, and the ability to break free from fear and the timid spirit our past and "shelters" create.

Diving Deeper:

Additional Scripture: Isaiah 43:18, 1 John 1:9

Name IT: Is there something in your past that is holding you back?

Claim IT: What is it?

Dump IT: Add to your Dump List a burden from the past you need to let go of in order to move forward. Prayerfully turn this burden over to God one day at a time.

P.E.A.C.E.

CYCLE THREE OF TEN

Waiting to be certain prior to taking action is a certain way of not getting anything accomplished. "Certainty" is best found by taking action.

Plan

3-Legacy Living

1 Samuel 2:10 (NIV), "He will give strength to his king and exalt the horn of his anointed."

*T*he first two chapters of 1 Samuel are quite interesting and include the story of Hannah, who for a long time was unable to have children. Hannah prayed persistently to God, asking for a child. She said if God blessed her with the ability to have a child, she would "give this child to the Lord for all the days of his life." God answered her prayers and blessed her with a child she named Samuel. Hannah fulfilled her promise to God and Samuel went on to anoint Saul and David, Israel's first two kings. What a legacy Hannah left behind because of her faith and keeping her promise to God.

Have you ever thought about your legacy? Do you realize everything you do creates a "wake" behind it? Are your actions focused on making a difference? Do you turn your life over to God all the days of your life like Hannah did, or are you totally consumed with the day-to-day living of making yourself feel good or trying to get ahead of, or simply keeping up with the Joneses? Is your wake a positive or negative wake?

This whole "legacy thing" came to me during my morning run after my devotion in Samuel. I was listening to the song, "Your Life is Now," by John Mellenkamp. I heard the lyrics, "Would you teach your children to tell the truth? Would you take the high road if you could choose? Do you believe you're a victim of a big compromise?" Listening to this song created a flashback in my mind. . . .

Years ago, after I had survived my brush with death because of the hole I had created in my stomach due to my lifestyle, I was meeting with the surgeon who had saved my life. He was explaining to me how close I came to dying because of the perforated duodenal ulcer. He then said something to me that I will never forget as he looked me in the eyes and said, "Jay you've got two children (this was before Michelle was born) and they need their dad. You need to change the way you are living."

He knew what was going on, although he said nothing about my life as an addict. In essence he was saying, "Your legacy is sucking right now and what you will leave behind if you don't change is a life of sorrow for your kids and a world that will be no different because of your existence."

That appointment with the surgeon took place four months before I took my last drink and drug. He will never realize how powerfully his words rang with me back in the spring of 1987. "Jay, your kids need their dad."

Since I got sober, I've been trying to keep my wake purposeful for my family and the world, one day at a time. I've been trying to "teach my children to tell the truth" through the way I live my life.

Diving Deeper:

Additional Scripture: 1Timothy 3:2-7, Proverbs 22:1, 1Timothy 6:17-19

Name IT: How is your wake/legacy going to look when you are gone?

Claim IT: What is the number one behavior that is "messing up" your wake?

Dump IT: Add this behavior to your Dump List and prayerfully turn it over to God one day at a time.

Effort

3-Letting Go

Philippians 3:13-14 (NIV), "But one thing I do: Forgetting what is behind and straining toward what is ahead I press on toward the goal to win the prize for which God has called me heavenward in Christ Jesus."

In our daily life we generally have three periods of time we live in; the past, the present, and the future. In my years of working with people with addiction and co-dependency problems, I have found a common trait to be that of procrastination. Procrastination is born out of having a fear of the future because of an inability to overcome the fears created by the past. This type of living causes us to get "stuck" in the present." As we all know, fear is from the devil and he enjoys observing us standing in place and doing nothing, especially if we profess to be Christians.

In Philippians 3, Paul, the former persecutor of the followers of Jesus' teachings, tells us to forget about the past and press on toward what is ahead. . .if Paul is able to let go of the past, then all of us should be able to do the same.

Many years ago when I was in my last quarter of my last year of pharmacy school, I had to present a case study to a group of doctors and colleagues at a hospital where I was doing a clinical rotation. The presentation was to be thirty minutes long. I had spent hours researching and compiling information to present my case in an excellent way. This was the first time I had ever spoken "publicly." To make a long story short, the minute I started to speak, I began stuttering and getting stuck on words. . .I stuttered and stammered for thirty minutes and bullets of sweat were rolling off of my forehead throughout the presentation. I was never so embarrassed in all my life.

Here I am, many years later, and most of my life is spent presenting and speaking to others. It comes to me "almost" naturally. The reason I used quotations around the word *almost*, is because today I always ask God to speak through me when I speak with or to others. Whenever I have a big presentation, I ask God to give me His words and to help me present them in His way, and it always seems to work out.

How many times have we let our fears from the past prevent us from receiving future blessings? If past experiences are not useful for today's living, then "let go and let God." If you are one of those who are unable to let go, then try the Twelve Steps or seek counseling. Life is simply too short to spend your time stuck in the present because of past fears that are preventing future blessings.

Another thing to keep in mind is the fact that God did not send his son to die for our sins so we can just sit still and do nothing. If you are one of those who call yourself a Christian, but spend the majority of your time dwelling on past sins or inadequacies, it is time to tap into the power of Christ and start living forward. Later in Philippians 4:13, *Paul gives us the key when he says: "For I can do everything through Him (Christ), who gives me strength."* (NIV) The key is giving "it" to Him and seeking His strength.

Where are you today? Are you "stuck" in the present? Although it takes effort and persistence, try practicing what it says in Philippians and let go and press on with a life powered by Jesus instead of fear one day at a time.

Diving Deeper:

Additional Scripture: Matthew 6:33, Philippians 4:13, Proverbs 12:25

Name IT: Do you have fears from past experiences that have you stuck in the present?

Claim IT: Which of these fears causes the most procrastination in your life?

Dump IT: Add this fear to your Dump List and prayerfully turn it over to God one day at a time.

Attitude

3-An Attitude of Faith in God's World

Romans 8:28 (NIV), "And we know that in all things God works for the good of those who love him, who have been called according to his purpose."

Many years ago, when my son Jordan was born and was not expected to make it, I found myself angry with God. Jordan was born during the height of my drug addiction/alcoholism days. At that point in my life, I believed in God but I only viewed him as being there for me when I needed Him. He was a God of "convenience" for me, and all of a sudden this God of "convenience" had turned his back on me; or so I thought.

I felt like God was punishing my child, and in turn punishing me for the life I was living. Jordan's situation created a make or break point in my life, and for the first eighteen months of his life I literally "broke." I took my addiction to another level as I medicated the pain and ran from the responsibilities that came from having a developmentally disabled child.

Long story short. . .Jordan's experience led me to Jesus. Although it was not easy and I lost virtually everything and had to start over, I can look back on that time and know the words of Paul in Romans 8:28 are true: ". . .in all things we know that God works for the good of those who love him."

For those of us who've suffered through tragic situations first hand, it is sometimes very difficult to see any good in the situation. But once through it, and with the help of God, we eventually see and experience the good.

As human beings, it is real easy to get stuck in the "world" and its ways and fail to experience what eternal life really is. Living eternally is more than just accepting Jesus and going to heaven. Living eternally means living the way Jesus encourages us to live in the here and now. Living eternally in the here and now also requires us to see the big picture and understand we do not have all the answers to why things happen, and that is why God created the word **"FAITH."**

God is a big God. God rules over all humanity. God is the alpha and the omega. God developed the divine plan. God developed the universe. God owns everything. God loves us so much he came down to earth and suffered a horrible death so we could be free of the bondage of sin. My faith serves me well, as I believe all of this.

But why does God allow tragedy to happen? Today, my **faith** tells me God obviously doesn't view tragedy the way the world does.

The best way to even begin to understand why tragedy happens is to get unstuck from the world's way of thinking and get *"stuck in the Word."* In Romans, Paul talks about how we can grow our faith, **"Consequently,** *faith* **comes from hearing the message, and the message is heard through the word of Christ."** (Romans 10:17 NIV)

If you are struggling with your faith and constantly find yourself asking God why something is happening, get into the gospels (Matthew, Mark, Luke and John) and not only read, but take the time to sit, pray, and "hear" the word of Christ.

Other ways of growing your faith by "hearing the words of Christ" is to attend church regularly and interact with others who are strong in their faith. Last but not least, extending a hand to others in need is an awesome way to experience and hear the words of Christ without uttering a word.

The bad news is faith doesn't "happen" overnight. The good news is it happens much more quickly when we are doing the things we need to do to quit listening to the world and instead listen to Christ.

Slowly but surely, the "WHYS" from any and all situations turn into one big "HOW". . .How can I grow from this experience and become a better disciple of the Lord?

Reminder. . .the whole faith walk journey is a process and not an event. It only takes two steps to be successful at it: Start and Continue.

P.S. Since 1986, Jordan has given our entire family and most people he comes in contact with an infinite amount of peace, joy, and happiness without ever speaking a word. Now, that is how having faith in God's world works.

Diving Deeper

Additional Scripture: Psalm 121:1-8, John 13:7, Matthew 17:20

Name IT: Do you find yourself having faith only when it is convenient and needed by you?

Claim IT: If so, why is this?

Dump IT: Add the "why" from above to your Dump List and prayerfully turn it over to God one day at a time.

Community

3-Help-ability and Community

Proverbs 1:22, 32-33 (NIV), "How long will you simple ones love your simple ways?

Proverbs 1:32-33 (NIV), "For the waywardness of the simple will kill them and the complacency of fools will destroy them; but whoever listens to me will live in safety and be at ease, without fear of harm."

For years I thought I had all the answers, and those answers got me a five-week "vacation" in a chemical dependency center, a "heart to heart" with an agent from the Drug Enforcement Administration (DEA), and the loss of almost everything I had by the time I was twenty-eight years old.

In the last couple of years of my addiction, I found myself un-help-able and un-teachable because I found my answers in my drugs. . .can you say, "wayward, simple and complacent?" (See the Proverbs verses above)

In chapter one of Proverbs, Solomon is being kind by using the word "simple" instead of stupid. What he is really saying is stupid people do stupid things and in turn reap the consequences of "stupid."

In my years of working with addicts and alcoholics, as well as people simply trying to improve, I have found those who are willing to be helped and taught are less likely to be "stupid," and in turn achieve one goal after another. Those who don't like to be helped, told, taught, or corrected are more likely to be "stupid" and remain stuck in a vicious cycle *their* answers have created.

When I decided to try to get my life back on track in the fall of 1987, I made a decision to spend at least a year seeking out the answers instead of providing them. I chose to take the cotton out of my ears and I placed it in my mouth. I sought out wise counsel through addiction counselors and mentors who had been where I was. I began attending Twelve Step self-help meetings. I began reading self-help books. . .I started becoming help-able and teachable, and in turn slowly found my actions to be purposeful and productive instead of stupid and foolish. . . Proverbs 12:15; "The way of a fool seems right to him, but a wise man listens to advice."

Putting forth productive effort requires a keen knowledge of what you are trying to produce. This only happens by being willing to be taught and in turn admitting you don't have all the answers. It also requires the humility to seek help from someone above your knowledge zone, whether you can meet with them in person or through their writings. (I assume business and life gurus like John Maxwell, Jim Collins, and Stephen Covey would probably not take my call for help, and that is why I read their books.)

If you want to put forth productive effort as a husband, seek advice and learn from a great husband. If you want to put forth productive effort as a mother, seek advice from a great mother. If you want to be the best at your job, seek help from a co-worker who is considered the best. If you want to overcome a nasty addiction, seek advice from someone who's overcome a nasty addiction. If you want to get in shape physically, seek advice from someone who is in shape physically.

All of the advice above is sound advice and will help you, but I have found the most effective way to put forth productive effort in ALL aspects of my life is to seek help from and remain teachable to the One person who walked among us and did not error. To remain teachable to the One who overcame the biggest setback any of us face as human beings (death), and to remain teachable to the One who has all the answers: "I am the way and the truth and the life." (Jesus is speaking in John 14:6 NIV.)

Years ago, when I made up my mind to seek the answers that would prevent me from being simple and stupid, I was lead to the One who held the answers for everything, and that One is Jesus.

Try turning to the ultimate teacher for answers to all your questions and begin to feel the "ease" Solomon talks about in Proverbs 1:33.

Diving Deeper

Additional Scripture: Proverbs 27:17, Proverbs 24:6

Name IT: Do you fall short in seeking guidance and help from others?

Claim IT: If so, why?

Dump IT: Add this "why" to your Dump List and prayerfully turn it over to God one day at a time.

Energy

3-Using outlets to "please" self and God

Romans 12:1 (NIV), "Therefore, I urge you, brothers, in view of God's mercy, to offer your bodies as living sacrifices, holy and pleasing to God—this is your spiritual act of worship."

I love to exercise and compete in sports, as they serve as great outlets for me and help to keep me not only physically fit but also mentally stable.

After years of playing basketball and using that as my outlet, I found my knees could no longer take the pounding, so I searched for a replacement, and several years ago I became a triathlete. Competing in triathlons serves as an awesome healthy outlet for me and creates positive energy for all aspects of my being. My training regimen, although quite intense, gives me more energy, a better attitude, and requires discipline that often bleeds into other areas of my life.

On top of all of this is the fact that spending time with other triathletes on race day is an uplifting experience for me because triathletes are quite focused and very positive people.

When I was in my downward spiral of addiction, I no longer had the desire to work out and exercise, even though it had been a major part of who I was. Addiction literally takes everything we once loved away from us (another topic for another day). My outlet had turned from exercise to getting high.

Once I got into recovery I learned from my counselors how important it would be for me to have an outlet for my mental energy, and exercise once again became a major part of my life as well as my recovery program.

Healthy outlets are an important part of living a healthy life and are especially important for those of us in recovery. How do you fill your "free" time today? Do you have an outlet? Is your outlet creating positive results? Is it pleasing to you and God?

A healthy outlet should create positive energy for most aspects of our lives, especially our roles with faith, family, work, and recovery. The litmus test of whether or not your outlets are effective is to ask yourself (honestly) if your outlet would be considered "pleasing" in the eyes of the Lord, as Paul points out in the scripture above.

Diving Deeper

Additional Scripture: 1 Corinthians 6:19, John 2:21

Name IT: Do you believe having a healthy outlet is critical to being all God wants you to be?

Claim IT: Do you have a healthy outlet? If not, what is standing in your way?

Dump IT: Add the healthy outlet barrier from above to your dump list and prayerfully turn it over to God one day at a time.

P.E.A.C.E.

CYCLE FOUR OF TEN

Anyone can be successful at the expense of others. It takes a special type of person to become successful for the benefit of others.

Plan

4-God's Plan/My Plan

John 16:33 (NIV), "I have told you these things, so that in me you may have peace. In this world you will have trouble. But take heart! I have overcome the world."

*E*very other year I speak to a hundred or so Covington 5th and 6th graders and high school students at the *Annual Covington 5th and 6th Grade Overnighter*. I was one of the founders of this event that started in 1988. I was about six months sober at the time and I thought it would be worth a try to prevent others from taking the path I had taken with drugs and alcohol by having a weekend event that promoted healthy decision-making.

The primary point I drive home with the students is the fact (barring any uncontrollable tragedies and illnesses) that we become the decisions and choices we make in our life.

Over the years, I have found that **great people** (people who achieve worthwhile goals that positively impact themselves and others) usually make **great decisions** the majority of the time. Great people also understand they own their choices and they don't let other negative people, places, and things interfere with their decision-making process.

I've also found that there are a lot of people who *could* be great but "choose" not to be because they allow negative people, places, and things to control their decisions.

One of the biggest obstacles (i.e., "things") that get in the way of people becoming great is their past. I know people who've allowed something that someone said years ago to paralyze them for life. Or maybe something negative happened in our past that "proved" to us we could never be great, and in turn we settle for a life of mediocrity or less.

Jesus tells us in the passage from John above that we will have trouble in this world, and in turn the world can control us if we choose to let it. He also tells us He has overcome the world and in Him we may have peace no matter what the circumstance.

In other words, reaching out to Jesus through the Holy Spirit will take us to a peaceful "state," away from the world, and in turn give us the ability to envision and become the great person God intends for us to be. **Jeremiah 29:11 (NIV), "For I know the plans I have for you," declares the Lord, "plans to prosper you and not to harm you, plans to give you hope and a future."**

It is your choice whether or not you want to become great. God has plans for you and these plans are not intended to harm you, but to give you hope and a future.

Let go of the world and the "things" that are harming you and getting in the way of your greatness, grab hold of God through the power of the Holy Spirit, and in turn take control of your decisions and your future today!

Diving Deeper

Additional Scripture: Romans 16:17, Ephesians 6:13, Isaiah 7:14-15

Name IT: Are there people, places, and things in your past that are roadblocks to gaining everything God wants you to have?

Claim IT: If so, name the biggest obstacle.

Dump IT: Add the obstacle to your Dump List and prayerfully turn it over to God one day at a time.

Effort

4-Excuses

Proverbs 22:13 (NIV), "The sluggard says, there is a lion outside." or, "I will be murdered in the streets."

We all have defining moments in our life. I feel blessed to have many that have taken me to where I am today. All throughout our life God places certain people in our path who, when listened to, will help take us to another level.

This was the case for me and my college basketball coach. My coach was stern, disciplined, and a very hard worker. I was happy-go-lucky, undisciplined, and worked hard only when I liked what I was doing. Next to my mom and dad, I learned more about productive effort from my college coach than anyone else in my life.

At the beginning of my junior year of basketball, I was projected to make all conference but got off to a very rough start. This was also my third year of pharmacy school, and pharmacy school was becoming quite challenging. I found myself drained of energy most of the time because I was doing nothing but playing basketball and studying.

Early in the basketball season, I could tell the coach was beginning to lose confidence in me as my game was beginning to digress. So I thought I had better meet with the coach and let him know why.

We met and I told him I knew my game was not where it should have been, but it would soon get better because I was going through a very difficult quarter in pharmacy school and the quarter was about to end.

He looked at me and said, "Jay, excuses are like our hind ends (actually used a different word for hind end), we all have them and they all stink," and then he walked out of the room.

Man, was I pissed off.

Today, I am so glad my coach said that to me because excuses truly do stink and will do nothing but get in the way of the attainment of our dreams and goals. I've referenced that moment with my coach many times over the years when I was struggling with a situation where I had more excuses than solutions.

I've worked with people in recovery as well as the business and basketball world for years, and the people who work hard and put forth a quality effort that equates into success very seldom waste time on excuses.

I know people who've been horribly abused as children and could only find solace through drinking and drugging, and eventually became alcoholics and/or drug addicts because of their inability to handle the pain of the past without medicating it. Some of these people have an epiphany and get sober and stay sober, while others don't. The primary reason (next to finding God) some are able to stay sober is they were able to let go of their past and quit using their past as an excuse every time things didn't go their way or obstacles were thrown in their path.

I can remember when I first got sober. I was trying to blame everything and everybody for the mess I was in (no money, facing jail time, and the loss of my professional license). Then my sponsor said to me one day, as I was "going off" about all the people who had screwed me and left me in this terrible state, "Jay, until you let go of the disappointments of the past there will be no future for you." And then he followed that up with the question: "Whose decision was it for you to drink and drug?"

Excuses are like our hind ends, they really do stink. Letting go of the past, as well as the excuses created in the past, is vital in being able to put forth productive effort in the attainment of our goals and dreams.

As Solomon so eloquently states in the Proverb above, excuses turn into frightening lions and we turn into sluggards. Do you suppose Satan is the gatekeeper of excuses?

Diving Deeper

Additional Scripture: Luke 9:59-62, Luke 14:18-20, Exodus 4:10-14

Name IT: Do you often make excuses to not have to do something or try something new?

Claim IT: What is your number one excuse?

Dump IT: Add the excuse from above to your Dump List and prayerfully turn it over to God one day at a time.

Attitude

4-The "Solution Attitude"

2 Corinthians 12:7-10 (NIV), "To keep me from becoming conceited because of these surpassingly great revelations, there was given me a thorn in my flesh, a messenger of Satan, to torment me. Three times I pleaded with the Lord to take it away from me. But he said to me, 'My grace is sufficient for you, for my power is made perfect in weakness.' Therefore I will boast all the more gladly about my weaknesses, so that Christ's power may rest on me. That is why for Christ's sake, I delight in weaknesses, in insults, in hardships, in persecutions, in difficulties. For when I am weak, then I am strong."

The great philosopher, Pogo, of the cartoon section in the newspaper, once said, "We have found the enemy and he is us." I thought of this one night a few years ago as I listened to a friend give her testimony at our recovery service at Ginghamsburg Church in Tipp City, Ohio.

She sought relationship "cures," chemical "cures," as well as geographical "cures" for her problems, but the problem continued to follow her, until one day she named the problem and the problem was her.

I learned a long time ago that a problem remains a problem as long as we stay in it. It always amazes me how quickly the problem disappears when we begin to live in the solution. Those of us in the recovery community who have found recovery and are living a new life, realized at some point that until we named our problem (us), there was never going to be a solution.

In essence, a life full of problems is a life fueled by self instead of God. Some great indicators of a life fueled by self, include being in constant turmoil, arguments, confrontations, worry, regret, fear, revenge, and envy; to name a few. I know some people who are always at war with something. . .can you relate?

I can remember a few years back when I found that the husband of a former employee of mine was diagnosed with terminal brain cancer and had only weeks to months to live. He had been diagnosed with the cancer three years earlier, and it looked as though his treatments were working until this latest report.

The family kept us all abreast with his valiant fight against the cancer through a website via the Internet. The family was deeply grounded in their Christian faith, and from the very first post they made on their website it was easy to tell they were choosing to live in *The Solution* and not the problem, as they referred to "God's will" early and often.

We are talking about a young couple with two little boys and many hopes and dreams for the future. It would seem to me that they would have every reason in the world to complain about their problems.

In one of her final posts prior to her husband's passing, the wife tells us that her husband says to her more than once, on the long car ride home from the hospital, "I'm going to get to see God soon." She closes her web post with the powerful words from Paul in 2 Corinthians 12:9; "But he (the Lord) said to me, 'My grace is sufficient for you, for my power is made perfect in your weakness.' Therefore I will boast all the more gladly about my weaknesses, so that Christ's power may rest on me."

What awesome witnesses for The Solution! Challenge yourself to get out of self and into "The Solution," which in turn allows your weaknesses to be turned into strengths for others to draw from.

Diving Deeper

Additional Scripture: Romans 5:3, Mark 4:17, Psalm 25:17

Name IT: Do you find yourself often living in problems instead of living in the solutions?

Claim IT: If you answered "yes" to the above question why is it you tend to live in the problem instead of the solution?

Dump IT: Add the above "why" to your Dump List and prayerfully turn it over to God one day at a time.

Community

4-What is life?

James 2:8 (NIV), "If you really keep the royal law found in Scripture, 'Love your neighbor as yourself,' you are doing right."

Albert Einstein once said, "A life lived for others; is a life worthwhile." I say "Amen" to good old Albert.

A mantra I try to live by is, "Live a lot, Love a lot, Laugh a lot and Give more than you got."

Back in my dark days when I was immersed in addiction and depression, I could not do any of this. I was so self-absorbed and self-consumed that I could not laugh and couldn't have cared less if I lived or not. I was consumed with "giving" myself that all-elusive high, and through my self-destructive habits, love was nowhere to be found. My life was all about me.

Then I found Jesus. And what I found in Jesus was a friend and Lord and savior who paid the ultimate price so I could have a second chance. This relationship with Jesus helped me forgive myself and learn how to live this life for not only myself, but for others. And that, my friends, is what this life is all about.

All throughout the gospels of the New Testament, Jesus tells us to love and give. The Twelve Step groups I was attending when I first got sober taught me a lot about loving and giving. Addiction, alcoholism, co-dependency, and depression are all self-focused disorders, and to get well we are told to get out of ourselves and help others.

As I slowly started to love and give to others, I found myself better able to live and laugh. The simple act of getting out of me and putting the attention on others became a life-transforming process. Today, loving and giving are second nature to me, but it took a lot of work, effort, and repetition to get where I am.

Where are you today? What is life to you? Do you find yourself thinking of yourself and your problems more than thinking about how you can make a difference in other people's lives? Try getting out of yourself by taking an interest in others or by taking an interest in a cause. You will be amazed at how this helps change your attitude and outlook on life.

(A disclaimer for the co-dependents: most of you become sick because you give way too much to others because your intent is to "fix" the other person or "create" an outcome. Try loving and giving with no strings attached, try doing for others without anticipating an outcome.)

Diving Deeper

Additional Scripture: John 15:12-13, Luke 18:18-25, Luke 10:30-37

Name IT: Do you struggle with giving and/or always loving your neighbor? Do you ever struggle with selfish behavior? When you do give of yourself, does it make you feel good?

Claim IT: When do you find it the most difficult to love and help someone?

Dump IT: Add the above thought to your Dump List and prayerfully turn it over to God one day at a time.

Energy

4-We have the ability to be smarter than Birds. . .

1 Peter 1:2-4 (NIV), "Grace and peace be yours in abundance through the knowledge of God and of Jesus our Lord."

Psalm 46:10 (NIV), "Be still, and know that I am God. . ."

I can remember a few years ago during my devotional time being joined by a beautiful red cardinal. From sunrise to sunset, my bird friend tried to fly into my study via the windows. He sat on a branch in a tree just outside the window, flew into the glass pane, and then "thud," he dropped to the ground, looked dazed and confused, but always flew back to the perch in preparation for his next mission. He did this all day long.

This bird is so symbolic of what many of us do with our lives, especially those who are battling any type of addiction or brokenness. We keep doing things the same way, expecting different results and the results never change (i.e., insanity). A bird, with its birdbrain, has an excuse for acting this way, but as human beings we have no excuse. Think of the energy wasted on doing the wrong things over and over and over!?

I know people who are miserable at this very moment because they are wasting energy trying to control something they have absolutely no control over, and most of the time what they are trying to control is either an addiction or another human being.

One of the best pieces of advice I received when I was in early recovery and working the first step was to not only say to myself that I was powerless over alcohol and drugs, but that I was powerless over other people, places, and things, and more importantly. . .I WAS NOT GOD.

I was also told to turn the things I was in turmoil about over to God on a daily or more frequent basis because

HE WAS GOD. *I can't, God can, I think I will let him*, is a saying I've used quite often during my recovery.

Choosing to no longer play God added an amazing amount of energy to my life. (Psalm 46:10)

Over the years, my morning-prayer and devotional time has allowed me to draw closer to God and farther away from things I have no control over. I've witnessed my former "birdbrain" transformed into a brain that allows me to discern quite rapidly what I can control (me and my thoughts, words, and deeds) and what I cannot control (other people, places, and things).

Where are you today? Are you trying to control things that are out of your control? Is this behavior zapping you of your energy? If so, try spending more time with God and less time with the people, places, and things in your head, and you will slowly begin experiencing grace, peace, and energy like never before. "Grace and peace be yours in abundance through the knowledge of God and of Jesus our Lord." (2 Peter 1:2 NIV)

<u>Diving Deeper</u>

Additional Scripture: Galatians 5:16-26, Hebrews 11:1

Name IT: Do you find yourself dwelling on things you have absolutely no control over?

Claim IT: List those things.

Dump It: Add the "uncontrollables" from above to your Dump List and prayerfully turn them over to God one day at a time.

P.E.A.C.E.

CYCLE FIVE OF TEN

Live life or life will live you.

Plan

5-Right Now

Jeremiah 29:11 (NIV), "For I know the plans I have for you declares the Lord, plans to prosper you and not harm you — plans to give you hope and a future."

One of my favorite rock songs of all time is *Right Now,* by Van Halen. Great tune with an awesome keyboard opening and powerful lyrics.

One of the greatest causes of the death of dreams is procrastination and paralysis from analysis. I learned a long time ago, if you are going to do something, then do it! That is what the *Right Now* lyrics keep saying over and over. . ."*Tell me what are ya' waitin' for?–turn this thing around. . .RIGHT NOW!*"

God does not give us the unique trait of imagination if he doesn't intend for us to turn our visions and dreams into reality.

Although procrastination is number one at preventing us from attaining our God dreams, there are many other "things" that get in the way of successfully acting upon our God dreams, and three of them seem to be more prevalent than the rest.

The first is fear, and like I've said many times in previous posts, fear is of the devil, and if the devil can get us to NOT chase our God dreams, then he wins. The best way to overcome fear is to put your faith in God and godly people, and not in other faces, places, and spaces that are driven by fear.

The second involves motives. Make sure whatever you dream and commit to doing is done to glorify God. I have found it is not very fun to have a God dream and then turn it into "Jay Dream." God gives us the ability to dream so that we can make a difference in His world. . .it is not our world. Turn your dream over to God on a daily basis and you will be amazed at what happens. I was part of turning a little corner drug store into a highly respected national company by giving it to God on a daily basis. Watching this business evolve from a staff of four employees to two hundred employees in the corn-fields of Covington, Ohio was nothing short of a God dream come true.

The third involves patience. Turning your God dream into reality takes time, effort, and perseverance. Thomas Edison failed over 1,000 times before effectively cre-ating the light bulb. Where would we be today if he had given up after his 999th try? The evolution of the busi-ness I referred to above began way back in 1982.

There is no dream or vision that is too big or too small to act upon. They all come together for the good if they are derived from and driven by God. Is there something special you want to do with your life? Is there something you are passionate about? Is there something you think about often? Is there something you picture yourself doing? Do you find yourself daydreaming about something, and then disregarding it as something stupid or too little or too big? I suggest you commit it to writing and get to work on it RIGHT NOW. . . .*tell me, what are ya' waitin' for?*

Diving Deeper:

Additional Scripture: 2 Timothy 1:7, Isaiah 41:10, Luke 1:37

Name IT: Do you have a God dream or goal that you are thinking about more often than not?

Claim IT: What is the God dream/goal?

Dump IT: What is standing in the way of allowing you to achieve your God dream? Add it to your Dump List and prayerfully ask God to assist you in working around, thru, below, or above it one day at a time.

Effort

5-Putting forth Effort and making our tomorrows better

James 1:21(NIV), "So get rid of all moral filth and the evil that is so prevalent and humbly accept the word planted in you, which can save you."

"All I want from tomorrow is to get it better than today," sang Huey Lewis in his song, "Jacob's Ladder," back in the late 80s. "Jacob's Ladder" is a spiritual song that reminds me of the step-by-step process of the Twelve Steps. The Twelve Steps, when *worked,* are a great way to rid ourselves of anything we are in bondage to. Bondage is anything that stands in the way of being all God wants us to be.

The Twelve Steps originated in Alcoholics Anonymous back in the 1930s, and have been utilized by various Twelve Step groups around the world to transform lives. The steps are a simple way to surrender to God, seek His help in overcoming our addictions, and clean up the wreckage of our past to be the best we can be, while helping God and others in the future.

The Christian Twelve Steps:

1. We admitted we were powerless over the effects of our separation from God, that our lives had become unmanageable.
2. Came to believe that a Power greater than ourselves could restore us to sanity.
3. Made a decision to turn our will and our lives over to the care of God, as we understood Him.
4. Made a searching and fearless moral inventory of ourselves.
5. Admitted to God, to ourselves, and to another human being the exact nature of our wrongs.
6. Were entirely ready to have God remove all these defects of character.
7. Humbly asked Him to remove our shortcomings.
8. Made a list of all persons we had harmed and became willing to make amends to them all.

9. Made direct amends to such people wherever possible, except when to do so would injure them or others.

10. Continued to take personal inventory, and when we were wrong, promptly admitted it.

11. Sought through prayer and meditation to improve our conscious contact with God, as we understood Him, praying only for knowledge of His will for us and the power to carry that out.

12. Having had a spiritual awakening as the result of these steps, we tried to carry this message to others and to practice these principles in all our affairs.

All of the steps are important and vital to live a happy, joyous, and free recovery life. The first three steps are all about "giving up" and surrendering to a power greater than ourselves (God/Jesus), steps 4 through 9 help us "clean up" the wreckage of the past and steps 10 thru 12 help us "grow up" and become responsible spiritual beings.

After Step 1 there is no step more important than the other.

To overcome whatever we are in bondage to, it is imperative to work the steps in the order they are written. Once the steps have all been worked, it is vital to do steps 10 thru 12 on a daily basis. Step 10 allows us to keep things "cleaned up" while steps 11 and 12 remind us of our powerlessness and the freedom we gain by practicing the steps in all our affairs and helping others.

Diving Deeper:

Additional Scripture: Luke 18:10-14, Luke 19:1-10, Luke 22:31-34

Name IT: Is there something separating you from God?

Claim IT: If so, is it mainly in your thoughts, words, and/or deeds?

Dump IT: Add all thoughts, words, and deeds separating you from God to your Dump List (if you haven't already done so over the past four weeks), and prayerfully turn them over to God one day at a time.

Attitude

5-The "Divine" Attitude Developer

Matthew 8:13 (NIV), "Go! It will be done just as you believed it would."

Many years ago, while attending a summer basketball camp, a motivational speaker talked with us about the importance of "visualization." He said: "What you picture yourself doing is what you will do."

Years after this camp, I read about this "self-fulfilling prophecy" concept in Napoleon Hill's book "Think and Grow Rich." In his book, Hill writes about how powerful our thoughts and pictures in our mind are. In essence, what we think about and picture ourselves doing. . .we will do.

I remember during my daughter's college basketball career, emailing her and reminding her of this concept. I did this after having a conversation with her and sensed she was dwelling on things she could not control, and there was a feeling of "fear of failure" in the tone of her voice. She was losing confidence in her game. I suggested she try to take ten minutes each day to visualize being the best at everything she could control, and to turn the pictures over to God for Him to "develop" them. She called me back a few days later and thanked me for the advice, because suddenly she was playing well again.

In the scripture from Matthew, Jesus was referring to a Centurion (a commander in the Roman army) who had approached Jesus in faith to have one of his servants healed. The servant was paralyzed and in terrible pain, and the Centurion had faith that Jesus would heal him. It is worth noting that the Jews hated the Roman centurions because of their dominant and controlling behavior, and it is safe to assume they figured there was no way Jesus was going to help this "nasty" person. But in this story, Jesus gives the Centurion a hand and heals his servant simply because the Centurion **believed** and **demonstrated this belief** by asking Jesus for help.

What are you "believing" these days? What are you spending time "looking at" in your head?

What you picture yourself doing and becoming is what you will do and become.

Most of the time, success and failure begin with your thoughts and the pictures in your mind. The pictures in your mind can produce very powerful results, whether they are positive or negative. . .it is your choice.

But even better yet, your pictures can be life-changing and transforming if you ask Jesus to "develop" them.

Diving Deeper:

Additional Scripture: Philippians 4:8, Romans 12:2, Matthew 12:33-37

Name IT:	Do you have a tendency of looking at the negative side of things? When do the negative thoughts take place?
Claim IT:	Where do these negative thoughts come from?
Dump IT:	Add all negative thoughts as well as their origin(s) to your Dump List and prayerfully turn them over to God one day at a time.

Community

5-Envy will rot your bones

Proverbs 14:30 (NIV), "A heart at peace gives life to the body, but envy rots the bones."

I don't know about you, but the thought of my bones rotting is a process that gives me a sick feeling. The Bible speaks the truth, as it is the living word of God. In the book of Proverbs, God speaks through Solomon and addresses many important life issues. Handling jealousy and envy is a gigantic life issue for all people, but especially alcoholics and addicts.

I can relate to my bones rotting because of envy or because of a heart that was not at peace.

Many years ago, I was facing death yet one more time. I had blown a hole in my stomach (i.e., perforated duodenal ulcer) and the acid from my stomach was pouring out into my abdominal cavity eating away at my organs. I was on vacation out in the middle of nowhere with no real hospitals within a twenty mile radius and the clock was ticking. I thought I was having a heart attack because the pain in my front quadrant was beyond excruciating.

After enduring six hours of this pain, with no relief in sight, I began asking the Lord to take me. I was dipping into shock and becoming very confused and hallucinating. A miracle saved me when a surgeon friend of ours diagnosed my condition over the phone from five-hundred miles away. Lori had called him at six in the morning out of pure desperation. His wisdom and a local surgeon's knife saved my life.

What is so crazy is the fact that I actually saw death as an easy way out, because no one would have known about the double life I had been living that led to this near-death experience.

During that period in my life I was obsessed with having as much as I could get. I couldn't work enough to get "things." As I reflect back on that time in my life, I also recall being jealous and envious of others who had what I wanted. I also recall a childhood of having to have the best of everything, and it drove me crazy if someone received more attention than I did. Jealousy was the order of the day for me. I would talk about people behind their backs, as I would do anything to bring them down. By the time I was twenty-eight, my body was "rotting."

Once I got on the right path, I began to understand the detrimental effects of a heart that is not balanced and at peace, of a heart that is constantly wanting what others have. . .coveting. I eventually figured out that if I became more concerned with what I could control, which was the planning of my life, my attitude and my work ethic, and my treatment of others, it no longer mattered what others had.

Today I am at peace most of the time because I not only control what I can control, but I ask God to help me control it.

In my years of working with alcoholics and addicts, one of the chief culprits of relapse is unattended envy and resentments. These feelings often kill us if we don't overcome them. Try living each day controlling what you can control, and allow God to run the show. You will be amazed at how quickly you quit worrying about what others have and how suddenly your life becomes peaceful, and you even become happy for the successes of others. We all have our own unique gifts, and it is our responsibility to maximize our gifts and appreciate and not envy the gifts God gives to others.

Paul tells us how to avoid the "rotting" process caused by envy in the 12th chapter of Romans (NIV) in the first six verses:

"Therefore, I urge you brothers, in view of God's mercy, to offer your bodies as living sacrifices, holy and pleasing to God — this is your spiritual act of worship. Do not conform any longer to the pattern of this world, but be transformed by the renewing of your mind. Then you will be able to test and approve what God's will is—his good, pleasing and perfect will.

"For by the grace given me I say to every one of you: Do not think of yourself more highly than you ought, but rather think of yourself with sober judgment, in accordance with the measure of faith God has given you. Just as each of us has one body with many members, and these members do not all have the same functions, so in Christ we who are many form one body, and each member belongs to all the others. We have different gifts, according to the grace given us."

Diving Deeper:

Additional Scripture: James 3:14-16, James 4:2-3, Proverbs 27:4

Name IT: Do you have days where your heart is not at peace and your body is suffering because of it?

Claim IT: What is getting in your way of having peace?

Dump IT: Add the "what(s)" from above to your Dump List and prayerfully turn them over to God one day at a time.

Energy

5-At the Core of the Olympics

Philippians 4:13 (NIV), "I can do all things through Him who strengthens me."

My wife and I are life-long athletes, and we always enjoy watching the Olympics and during the 2008 and 2012 Summer Olympics Michael Phelps etched his name into the record books of swimming for eternity. For those of you who watched the Olympic swim competitions in '08 and '12, did you happen to get a good look at Michael Phelps' abs? His core obviously had much to do with his success.

Years ago, I studied to become a personal trainer, and throughout that process I learned that the greatest athletes had the greatest balance, and balance was derived from having strong "core" muscles. It was explained to me that for the upper body muscles to work in perfect unison with the lower body muscles, the core muscles needed to be the strongest.

Well, believe it or not, some of the most energetic and effective people I know are also well balanced with a very strong core. Their core is strengthened by a personal relationship with Jesus Christ. Just as the great athlete's core muscles help the upper body muscles work in perfect harmony with the lower body muscles, the Holy Spirit serves the same purpose for us and allows us to have everything we do work in unison with God's will.

Just like an Olympic athlete, the "core" of a Christian gets strengthened by working it on a daily basis. Every morning I do my "core" spiritual exercises of prayer, devotion, meditation, and reading, and then my "core" physical exercises of various abdominal and upper leg exercises. Becoming alive with the Holy Spirit only requires one step. . .accepting Jesus as Lord and Savior. Becoming strengthened, energized, and ultimately balanced by the Holy Spirit is a daily walk.

How is your core?

Diving Deeper:

Additional Scripture: Hebrews 13:8, Psalm 28:7, Galatians 5:1

Name IT: Is your spiritual core as strong as it should be?

Claim IT: Why isn't it?

Dump IT: Add the answer from above to your Dump List and prayerfully turn it over to God one day at a time.

P.E.A.C.E.

CYCLE SIX OF TEN

Sin is not a metric to be used to measure and/or judge the lives of others. It is a metric to be used to measure and/or judge our own.

Plan

6-What's Your Season? and Defining Your Purpose

Ecclesiastes 3:1 (NIV), "There is a time for every-thing, and a season for every activity under heaven."

*S*omewhere around 1999, I decided to write my vision and mission statement for my life. It has nothing to do with personal success, but it helps me keep the "main thing the main thing."

My vision statement: "To be a positive difference maker in God's world in all my roles and responsibilities one day at a time."

My mission statement: "To live my life in a way that will glorify God and allow his light to shine through me in all I do."

What I found was my vision and mission statements were flexible no matter what the season was in my life.

Our purpose is often season-dependent.

It is okay to have a "purpose" focused on raising your kids the godly way during your child-raising season. Remember, you only have one shot at raising your kids if you have kids.

It is okay to have a purpose that entails getting sober and getting well.

It is okay to have a purpose focused on being the best spouse you can be.

It is okay to have a purpose where your work ethic represents God's light.

It is okay to have a purpose where you quietly help others in need.

What I have found is my purpose is season-dependent and my personal vision/mission statement allows the seasons and purposes to evolve as God's plan evolves. Many people get this messed up because they try to change and/or dictate their season, and then anxiety sets in and then focus is lost on what the "main thing" is. . .can you say Satan???

David, one of the Bible's strongest God characters, and a man with a purpose, says in Psalm 1:1-3 (NIV), *"Blessed is the man who does not walk in the counsel of the wicked or stand in the way of sinners or sit in the seat of mockers. But his delight is in the law of the lord, and on his law he meditates day and night. He is like a tree planted by streams of water, which yields its fruit in season and whose leaf does not wither. Whatever he does prospers."*

David is saying we will prosper by simply keeping the main thing the main thing. . .by planting our tree (our life) near water (God) and letting the tree yield fruit in "season." God has a season when He will fully reveal His ultimate purpose for us, but it will not and cannot be revealed if we are trying to create and/or change our seasons without God's direction. I believe He sees how we are handling our current seasons before He throws more responsibility and "purpose" at us.

Create a flexible vision/mission statement focused on God, and keep putting one foot in front of the other by keeping the main thing the main thing and when the season is right God will help you see your ultimate purpose. Remember, Moses was eighty years old and in his twilight "season" when he was given his ultimate purpose in life.

Diving Deeper:

Additional Scripture: Acts 1:7, Daniel 2:21, Revelation 12:14

Name IT: What season are you currently in, in your life? Are you handling it the way God would want you to handle it?

Claim IT: Are there things getting in the way of you making the most of this season?

Dump IT: Add anything that is getting in your way of making the most of the season your life is in to your Dump List and prayerfully turn it over to God one day at a time.

Effort

6-How may I help you, God?

Proverbs 19:21 (NIV), "Many are the plans in a man's heart, but it is the Lord's purpose that prevails."

Several years ago I can remember hitting a dry spell in my faith walk. No matter how many different ways I prayed and read scripture, it was like God wasn't listening or talking to me. I was seeking guidance about something in my life, and I kept getting nothing. A friend of mine shared with me the fact that God was probably allowing me to walk in the desert to motivate me to reach out more.

So I decided to reach out more. I increased my prayer time and even went to a total surrender position of being on all fours while praying. Then it happened. A couple of days ago during my prayer time, God spoke to me, and he said, "Jay, instead of asking for help from me, why not ask how you can help me?"

Sometimes we get so hung up on our own crap that we forget what we are here to do, and that is to be the hands and feet of God. A life run by EGO (Easing God Out) is a sure-fire way of allowing Satan to mess with our minds. Ego can manifest itself in so many different ways and can overtake us even when we are praying, reading scripture, and worshiping, especially when our prayer, reading, and worship are all focused on helping ourselves.

Ego wants us to put ourselves first. God tells us to love Him first and to love others like we love ourselves. If this is the way it is supposed to be, then there is no room for ego when it comes to living the Christian life.

I decided to go back to the basics and started praying the third step prayer from page 63, of the third edition of, "The Big Book of Alcoholics Anonymous," each and every morning. This is something I did in early sobriety, and for some reason got away from it. The prayer is short, sweet, and most of all "ego-deflating."

"God, I offer myself to Thee–to build with me and to do with me as Thou wilt. Relieve me of the bondage of self, that I may better do Thy will. Take away my difficulties, that victory over them may bear witness to those I would help of Thy Power, Thy Love, and Thy Way of life. May I do Thy will always!" AMEN

If you've been seeking God's help and you don't feel like He is responding, try asking God how you can be of help to Him. This life is not about our plans and hopes and dreams, it is about allowing God to live through them and in-turn bring others to Him.

Diving Deeper:

Additional Scripture: Philippians 2:1-10, 2 Corinthians 10:12

Name IT: Do you find that your requests of God outnumber your "quests" to help God's people?

Claim IT: What gets in the way of you being of help to God?

Dump IT: List those things that get in the way of you helping God and place them on your Dump List and prayerfully turn them over to God one day at a time.

Attitude

6-Attitude Go-Tos

Hebrews 6:19 (NIV), "We have this hope as an anchor for the soul, firm and secure."

I remember years ago during my basketball playing days when I had finally developed a "go-to" move offensively. A "go-to" move is a move that allowed me to separate myself from my defender and get a shot off no matter what the circumstance. Having this "go-to" move gave me confidence on the offensive end of the floor, because it gave me an out no matter how tough the defender was.

When I was at the pits of my life, I had no healthy "go-to." My "go-to" was me and my drugs, and these "go-to's" virtually destroyed me. During this period in my life, the only hope I saw was to run away from the disaster I had created. The only out I could see was to take my own life.

Then in a moment of "weakness," I turned to God and simply said, "Help Me!" The rest is history, albeit a sometimes rough and rocky history, but it has been much better than my previous ways.

Living a life that involves surrendering "all" to God on a daily basis is so much more pleasant than trying to do it all alone. No matter how crazy things are today, I always know there is hope in my "go-to" and that "go-to" is God, who serves as my *anchor and truly is firm and secure,* no matter what type of situation I am facing.

Recovery from anything that is separating us from the "hope and security" of God requires us to surrender everything we have to God, especially that which we are in bondage to. Surrender needs to take place at least daily or on a more frequent basis. . .sometimes hourly. . .until we finally get it.

Having hope requires a willingness for us to get out of the way to allow God to act not only as the answer, but as the numerator, the denominator, and as the sum of all parts. It requires us to have faith that **"we can do all things through Him who strengthens us." (Philippians 4:13)**

Today, when the chips are down, I know I have a "go-to" in God, and to reach Him quickly I have "go-to" phrases and scripture.

When I am tempted by Satan, I often say, "By the blood of Jesus, Satan be-gone." When I am having difficulties in handling life on life's terms, I often go to my "go-to" verse; **". . .but those who hope in the Lord will renew their strength. They will soar on wings like eagles; they will run and not grow weary, they will walk and not be faint." (Isaiah 40:31NIV)**

Jesus died for our sins for us to have a "go-to" in the Holy Spirit, which is God in us. As Christians, it is such a waste to not use the power and strength Jesus' death and resurrection provides to us in the Holy Spirit. We have a "go-to" for all situations and circumstances.

Living life on life's terms is not easy, but we have the ability to gain hope and comfort, no matter how uncomfortable the circumstance, if we tap into our "go-to." All it takes is a willingness to declare God as the "go-to" on a daily basis, and then go to Him as often as needed, and suddenly disaster and challenges turn into hope and opportunity. Been there, done that, and still doing it.

Oh, by the way, it took me hours and hours of practice to develop my "go-to" in basketball. It takes similar practice to develop a confidence in having a "go-to" in God. Challenge yourself to start practicing today.

Diving Deeper:

Additional Scripture: 1 Samuel 2:2, Hebrews 13:8, John 14:26

Name IT: Do you have a "go-to" when life becomes challenging? Is it healthy? Is it God?

Claim IT: List some unhealthy "go-to's" you need to stay away from.

Dump IT: Add the unhealthy "go-to's" from above to your Dump List and prayerfully turn them over to God one day at a time.

Community

6-Quit talking and start walking. . .

1 Corinthians 2:14 (NIV), "The man without the Spirit does not accept the things that come from the Spirit of God, for they are foolishness to him, and he

cannot understand them, because they are spiritually discerned."

Have you ever been involved in a conversation you couldn't care less about? You know the one where two or three people are talking with excitement and fervor, and you are standing there, saying to yourself, "I couldn't care less and even more why are they wasting my time talking about something I have no connection to?"

This is how I am with the sport of hockey. Even though I'm an old jock, for years I've said, "Hockey is not a sport." I refuse to watch it on TV or talk with anyone about it. I couldn't care less about hockey. I am sure it is a great sport, but that is just the way it is for me.

It is like talking about addiction to someone who has never had a problem with it and couldn't care less about it. (I found this to be true when I was in early recovery and shared with someone I hadn't drunk a beer for a year, and they looked at me and said, "So, what is the big deal? I never drank and never will.")

Something I learned early on in my faith walk is that not everyone cares about God like I do. I believe a big reason for the world's not so lustrous view of Christianity is that many Christians find God, they get saved, and then they try to stuff their beliefs down the throat of someone who couldn't care less.

This does not mean we aren't supposed to try to lead others to the Lord. What Paul is saying in 1st Corinthians above, is that those without the Spirit cannot speak our language, nor understand it.

But, as we all know, our actions speak much louder than our words.

When I was at my pits in life and was reaching for God and trying to find a better way, I thought about those around me who had it together, and most of them were Christians. It was at that moment I went to some of them with questions and they gave me answers. Why was I attracted to them? Because they had something I wanted. They were reaping the fruits of the Spirit. The funny thing about my situation was that this group of Christians knew I was in trouble, but none of them ever came to me and tried to stuff religion down my throat. But I noticed they always seemed to be "around." Later, they told me they were praying continuously for me and my family.

When I am asked to help someone who is struggling with an addiction, the first question I ask the addict is, "Do you believe in God?" I assess whether or not they will be able to "speak and hear the language." If they say, "Yes," then I know I can begin the process of explaining grace, mercy, forgiveness and the expansiveness of God's power to them. If they say "NO" I handle it a totally different way. In both instances, I try hard to let my actions speak much louder than my words, and I pray daily for the person in need. The ultimate goal is to lead the addict to the Lord.

Bottom line. . .prayer and walking the walk is much more powerful and attractive to the unbelievers than talk.

Diving Deeper:

Additional Scripture: James 1:26, 1 John 4:20, Matthew 6:1

Name IT: Take a moment and reflect on your walk today. Is it spent talking or is it spent walking? Leading others to God is more about attraction than it is promotion.

Claim IT: Are there things you do that are not a good representation of the life you are trying to live as a Jesus follower?

Dump IT: Add the things from above to your Dump List and prayerfully turn them over to God one day at a time.

Energy

6-Thy Will=More Energy

1 John 4:15, (NIV), *"If anyone acknowledges that Jesus is the son of God, God lives in him and he in God."*

I can remember the first time I read the above scripture and thought, "Wow, God sure did make it easy for us." All we need to do is acknowledge that Jesus is the son of God and God (the Holy Spirit) will live in us.

But just because we believe Jesus is the son of God and God is living in us does not mean all our challenges will disappear.

There is this thing called free will that God gives us. It is our decision (free will) whether or not we want God to run the show. For some people, letting God run the show is easy, but for me it is a daily walk. If I don't do certain things every day, then it is "self-will run riot" for this poor sap. I was the "strong-willed child" in our family. And when you get right down to it, running our life on self-will is quite draining to our energy bank.

I've witnessed a lot of Christians over the years who struggle with being at peace. They are always in search of something more. I was there several years ago and found that I was simply trying to have the best of both worlds. . .mine and God's. It doesn't work that way.

You see, there is no such thing as "life in between" with God; you are either in or out. Oh sure, he still loves us no matter what we do, but selectively asking God for help is a recipe for instability and possible disaster. There is not a worse place to be as a Christian than on the fence. . .and it really hurts your crotch area, if you know what I'm saying.

James talks about sitting on the fence in James 1:6-8 (NIV); *"But when he asks, he must believe and not doubt, because he who doubts is like a wave of the sea, blown and tossed by the wind. That man should not think he will receive anything from the Lord; he is a double-minded man, unstable in all he does."*

Divided loyalty between earth and heaven is a recipe for instability and is quite exhausting. Take the easy way out and give it all to God a day at a time.

Diving Deeper:

Additional Scripture: 1 John 2:16-17, Luke 6:46, Ephesians 5:15-20

Name IT: Are you often experiencing the end of your energy before your day is over?

Claim IT: What are you dwelling on that is getting in the way of serenity and in-turn taking your energy away from you?

Dump IT: Add the "what" from above to your Dump List and prayerfully turn it over to God one day at a time.

P.E.A.C.E.

CYCLE SEVEN OF TEN

Some of the greatest blessings in life occur after we
don't get what we want.

Plan

7-What's your PLAN?

Proverbs 16:3 (NIV), "Commit to the Lord whatever you do, and your plans will succeed."

*A*s a recovering person, I have found how important it is to have a daily **Plan.** My first sponsor was a stickler about carrying a calendar book at all times and planning each day the night before.

I really had a hard time with this in the beginning. I don't know if it was due to the fact I have a touch of

Attention Deficit/Hyperactivity Disorder (ADHD) or because I simply wasn't disciplined enough to do it.

Over the years, I have found a common denominator among those of us with addiction problems is a general lack of discipline coupled with immature behavior. (I was always good at being disciplined and mature when I was doing things I wanted to do. . .go figure. . .selfish, self- serving.)

Today, discipline means doing what God wants me to do, whether I like it or not. Thus the reason I ask him to guide my plans.

Another problem planning has helped me with is it has helped curtail the mood swings that many of us in recovery experience in the beginning. Having a plan assists me in staying off the pity pot by directing my energies outward instead of inward. Awakening in the morning to a plan leaves little time for the committee in my head to start conversing.

Today I carry a journal and in my journal is my Life Vision Statement, and I try to read my Vision Statement every day. I find that if my plans are derived from my

Vision Statement, I am a productive child of God. If they aren't, I become a wayward child of the World.

In my journal, I write a weekly plan on Sunday, and then throughout the week I summarize each day in the evening and create a plan for the following day. My journal also contains my morning devotional and evening summary for the day. It doesn't work perfectly, but it works for me. I always take time in late summer and early fall to reflect and draw direction from God on what direction my plans are to take for the following year.

If you often find yourself uptight, emotional, straying off the God path, or just plain unproductive, get a plan.

BUT — for those perfectionists out there, don't let the plan drive you crazy if you are unable to carry it out. There will be interruptions, setbacks, and just plain rewrites. But I have found I would much rather have a plan go wrong than to have no plan at all.

Diving Deeper:

Additional Scripture: Proverbs 13:16, Luke 14, 28-30, 2 Corinthians 1:17

Name IT: Do you work off of a plan? If so, do you commit your plans to the Lord? Or do you often do things by the seat of your pants?

Claim IT: If you do not plan, why not? What are the reasons for not having a plan?

Dump IT: Place your reasons for not planning on your Dump List and prayerfully turn them over to God one day at a time.

Effort

7-Sowing and Reaping

Malachi 3:10 (NIV), "Bring the whole tithe into the storehouse, that there may be food in my house. Test

me in this says the Lord almighty, and see if I will not throw open the floodgates of heaven and pour out so much blessing that you will not have room enough for it."

Sometimes I feel like God has used me as the poster child for proving his scripture is the truth. After I crashed and burned years ago, I took a look at my personal financial situation, and it was scary. Here I thought I was building a new empire, and all I was building was a hole of debt.

Because I was in so much financial trouble, the second order of business for this new Jesus follower (the first order was to pray daily for God to keep me sober) was to begin tithing. . .hey 10 percent of nothing is nothing, right?

I've got to be honest with you: I was testing God, I was desperate, and anything was worth a try. Although we are told to never test God, this is one area he **tells** us to test him, as written in Malachi above.

Many years ago, my wife and I decided we were going to give the first 10 percent of our fruits back to God. This was very difficult in the beginning, but we did it. We had decided that my way obviously wasn't working and why not give God a shot? After all, He is God.

So here we are, years later, truly feeling what it means when God says, "I will open the floodgates of heaven and pour out so much blessing that you will not have room enough for it."

Most people think the "blessing" he is talking about is monetary blessing, and some of it is. But the blessings come in various shapes and sizes. We've been blessed with stable children, unbelievable college educations for our kids, a stable income, a stable marriage, and a life of recovery that has brought thousands of people into our lives whom otherwise we would have never known. These are but a few of the eternal blessings we've experienced over the years.

One of the greatest blessings we received by turning our first fruits over to God was the desire to be debt-free.

Debt is of the devil because if he (the devil) can get us to spend what we don't have, then it will be even more difficult to give anything to God. Does that make sense? Debt creates a state of paying backwards instead of forward. We end up giving our first fruits to the devil, and that sucks!

As I said earlier, in some ways I believe God has used me as the poster child for proving his scripture is the truth. Today, my wife and I have no personal debt, including our homes, and we give 15 to 20 percent of our income back to helping God. I do not say this boastfully. I am saying it as a witness to what living God's word will do for your life.

There is a freedom that is a wonderful by-product of living debt-free and paying forward. One of my favorite books in the Bible is Galatians. Galatians speaks directly to those of us who struggle with addictions and the want of worldly possessions. In Galatians 6:7, Paul writes, *"Do not be deceived. God cannot be mocked. A man reaps what he sows. The one who sows to please his sinful nature, from that nature will reap destruction; the one who sows to please the Spirit, from the Spirit will reap eternal life. Let us not become weary in doing good, for at the proper time we will reap a harvest if we do not give up."*

To that I say Amen, Amen and Amen.

Diving Deeper:

Additional Scripture: Job 4:8, 2 Corinthians 6:15, Galatians 6:7

Name IT: Do you believe what the Bible says about sowing and reaping?

Claim IT: Are you sowing the way God instructs us to sow? If not, why?

Dump IT: Add to your Dump List the "why(s)" from above and prayerfully turn them over to God one day at a time.

Attitude

7-An Attitude of Possibility Thinking

Proverbs 17:22(NIV), "A cheerful heart is good medicine, but a crushed spirit dries up the bones."

Some time ago I had an interesting discussion via email with some friends as we openly debated an issue relevant to the Christian community worldwide. It always amazes me how much can be learned from others through candid discussion. After this exercise of point-counterpoint, I spent some time reflecting on why I always seem to find the positive side to everything, or the fact that I seem to thoroughly enjoy countering those who are representing what I consider negative points of view.

I remember seeing this quote somewhere years ago: "Jesus came to tell us what we could do, not what we couldn't do." In other words the law, although still a great resource to know right from wrong, was replaced by Jesus so we could have abundant life, i.e., eternal life, in the here and now, as well as the afterlife.

By accepting Jesus as Lord and Savior, we not only are forgiven of our sins and receive the free gift of eternal life, but if we follow His teachings we also reap the fruits of the Holy Spirit (Galatians 5:22-23 NIV), "love, joy, peace, patience, kindness, goodness, faithfulness, gentleness, and self-control."

Jesus wants us to experience peace and joy no matter what the circumstance. This is not easy, but once it becomes a habit life becomes so much more enjoyable, regardless of the situation. I've experienced a personal transformation of my own negativism turning into positivism and possibilities over the past several years, and it is a great way to not only live life, but to enjoy life.

As I reflect back on my career of coaching the teammates who worked for me at my business, I always painted a picture of, "This is what the customer and you will have if we do these things." When I coached my kids' AAU basketball teams, I always talked about, "This is what we need to do to win championships." During my kids' formative years, I always talked about, "This is what can happen if you do these things." When I talk to others about Jesus, I tell them, "This is what you will gain by following Jesus' instructions."

Painting a picture of possibilities creates drive and determination in human beings. When you are able to look at situations and see possibilities and opportunities instead of losses and negative consequences, you will win a lot more "games" in life than you lose.

The Proverb above tells it all; being positive and cheerful is good medicine and creates a winning formula, but **negativism breaks the spirit and dries a person's bones.**

If you struggle with negativism and always see the cup as "half-empty," challenge yourself to replace your can't-do statements with can-do's. Choose to hang with and interact with other "can-do" people (this includes what you read, as well as what you listen to on radio and watch on TV), and most importantly read, listen to, and follow the One who tells us what we **can do,** and that One is Jesus.

Diving Deeper:

Additional Scripture: Joshua 1:9, Proverbs 15:30, 2 Corinthians 4:17-18, Romans 8:37-39, Isaiah 60:1-3

Name IT: Is your cup "half-empty" or "half-full" most of the time?

Claim IT: If you are more negative than positive, what do you attribute this behavior to?

Dump IT: Add the reasons for your negativity to your Dump List and prayerfully turn them over to God one day at a time.

Community

7-The End

Luke 10:25-28 (NIV), "On one occasion an expert in the law stood up to test Jesus. 'Teacher,' he asked, 'what must I do to inherit eternal life?' Jesus replied, 'What is written in the Law? How do you read it?'

The expert answered: 'Love the Lord your God with all your strength and with all your mind and, Love your neighbor as yourself.' Jesus stated, 'You have answered correctly, do this and you will live.'"

Back in July of 2009, I can remember starting my day doing something no dog owner ever wants to do. I had to bury our fourteen-year-old lab/chow, Jasmine. What a great dog! As I shoveled the last bit of dirt on her grave during a steady rain that morning, I couldn't help but get a little emotional. The death of our dog was the sixth death of someone I considered a friend or fairly close acquaintance since my buddy Joe died on April the 14th, just three months earlier. What a year that was as far as death goes, and I can remember challenging myself to make sure I was living and loving as much as I could. None of us know when "the end" will come.

It was also during the summer of 2009 that my family was blessed with the opportunity to see Paul McCartney perform the first-ever concert at the New York Mets new stadium, Citi Field in New York City. The Beatles had performed their first ever outdoor-stadium concert at the old Mets stadium (Shea Stadium) some forty-four years earlier.

All members of the Meyer family are Beatle fans, and we all enjoyed an unbelievable, historic evening together. Although sixty-seven years old at the time, Paul McCartney still rocked and sang like no other. He sang for almost three hours, did two encores, and surprised us all by having Billy Joel jump on the stage and play the piano during, "I Saw Her Standing There."

One of my all-time favorite Beatle songs is the grand finale on their last album, *Abbey Road*. The name of the song is, "The End." The song has a pretty cool solo drum piece by Ringo, as well as solo guitar pieces by George, Paul and John.

Paul's final song that Friday evening (at the end of the second encore) was, "The End."

I thought about the last line of the lyrics in "The End" as I was burying Jasmine that damp summer morning back in 2009: **"and in the end, the love you take is equal to the love you make."** Jasmine took a lot of love to her grave with her because she created a lot of love in our lives. Then I thought about the finality of death. . .death is "The End" of our earthly life. Then I thought, "Am I loving enough?"

Although as Christians, death is the beginning of a new era for us, God put us on this earth to do more than just live and die. He wants us to find Jesus and help others find Jesus, but on an equivalent path, He wants us to love one another. He wants us to love unconditionally despite race, religious beliefs, sexual preferences, addictions, likes, dislikes, looks, economic class, etc. . .sort of like how a dog loves.

In fact, in Luke 10:25-28, Jesus tells us that love is a prerequisite for eternal life. I believe eternal life is not just about what we do after we die. We can experience the fruits of eternal life in the here and now if we choose to love.

What is your love towards other people like today? Does it come with conditions? If "The End" came about tomorrow, how much love will you take with you?

Amazing what questions the Spirit can stir up by simply burying a dog. A dog that was obviously full of love.

Diving Deeper:

Additional Scripture: John 3:16, 1 Peter 4:8, 2 Peter 1:7-8

Name IT: What is your love towards other people looking like these days? Is it unconditional, or are you selective? If "The End" came about tomorrow, how much love will you take with you?

Claim IT: If you feel as though you aren't "loving" as much as God wants you to; then why aren't you?

Dump IT: Add the "why" from above to your Dump List and prayerfully turn it over to God one day at a time.

Energy

7-No Turning Back

1 Corinthians 9:24-27 (NIV), "Don't you realize that in a race all the runners run, but only one gets the prize? Run in such a way as to get the prize. Everyone who competes in the games goes into strict training. They do it to get a crown that will not last; but we do it to get a crown that will last forever. Therefore I do not run like a man running aimlessly; I do not fight like a man beating the air. No, I beat my body and make it my slave so that after I have preached to others, I myself will not be disqualified for the prize."

A huge part of my life today involves doing things that generate energy (i.e., prayer, eating right, sleeping right, and exercising). The more energy I have, the better chance I have in effectively taking on the challenges of the day and accomplishing my goals as well as God's.

Several years ago, I started competing in triathlons as I knew if I had a reason to train I would be more disciplined in my eating, sleeping, and exercising habits. Competing in triathlons gives me the opportunity to stretch my body to limits I once never thought imaginable, and it also gives me a natural peace to my mental state, which is always needed.

Triathlons involve swimming, biking, and running total distances of anywhere from sixteen to 140 miles. . .dependent on how crazy you are.

Back in June of 2010, I had the opportunity to spend my Father's Day with my oldest son in Washington, D.C., competing in the inaugural D.C. Triathlon. I must admit we were both a little nervous about the swim, as it involved swimming in the Potomac River. We both had experience in swimming in lakes and pools, but never a huge body of water with only two boundaries and an undercurrent like the Potomac, plus the swim started at 5:30am. The good news is there were 3,500 other "crazies" in their swim gear at 5:30am, getting ready to do the same thing.

It all came down to trusting our abilities to swim, because once in the water there was no turning back, and yes, my son and I had decided before the race that it was "game on," and "may the best triathlete win."

Prior to the race, we were reminiscing about the many times we had competed against each other in the past. I used to crush him in Candy Land, but then he got revenge in Memory (I had an excuse, because the drugs had burned my memory), and we both chuckled as we recalled the many epic one-on-one basketball battles in our backyard.

Walking the Christian walk is quite similar to competing as an athlete, as Paul so eloquently states in 1 Corinthians. It takes discipline (the bridge between goals and success) to train our body and mind to do what it takes to be prepared to do what God wants us to do and in turn have "purpose in every step."

Disciplining ourselves as Christians involves the daily routine practice of scripture reading, constant contact with God through prayer and meditation, interaction with accountability partners, weekly worship, and opening our hands to others. . .to name a few. Eventually this practice develops into a habit, and then when we are faced with a tough decision of whether or not we will continue to "swim" or turn back, we will trust our instincts (i.e., the Holy Spirit) and continue on and do what we've trained ourselves to do. A true Christian walk means there is no turning back, as our daily disciplines and faith keep propelling us forward.

Although we had some fear going on as we looked at the Potomac while the sun was beginning to rise over the Washington Monument, we trusted our instincts that told us we had trained and prepared ourselves well enough to take on the battle; and that we did.

Even though I was battling age and my son was battling dehydration, we finished the race strong and crossed the finish line together, which simply means we both know today there is a bigger and better race we are running, one which involves an eternal prize.

Diving Deeper:

Additional Scripture: Nehemiah 5:14-16, Romans Chapter 11, Romans 12:1-2,

Name IT: Are you running your "race" in a way God would want you to run it? Do you try your best to be all in, with a "no turning back" attitude?

Claim IT: Do you run part of your "race" as a Christian and other parts as an atheist (i.e., in ways unbecoming of a Christian)? If so, then why?

Dump IT: Add the "why" from above to your Dump List and prayerfully turn it over to God one day at a time.

P.E.A.C.E.

CYCLE EIGHT OF TEN

If you want to be something different, start thinking something different.

Plan

8-Running with a purpose...

1 Corinthians 9:24 (NIV), "Do you not know that in a race all the runners run, but only one gets the prize? Run in such a way as to get the prize."

O ne of my favorite self-help books is, "The 7 Habits of Highly Effective People," by Stephen Covey. Next to the Bible, it is the one book I've read more than any other. The Third Habit in Covey's book is "Putting First Things First." I believe this habit is what separates those who achieve their goals from those who don't.

Putting first things first means we prioritize our lives, and then our various goals become by-products of what is important to us. It is easier to deny ourselves of things when we know where our priorities are.

For example, as a part of my priority to be fiscally responsible, I have a goal of staying debt-free, and to do that I deny myself the urge to buy a second home in a warmer place than Ohio.

My number one priority is to stay sober by growing closer to Jesus. Because of this, the first thing I do every day is pray and read the Bible and deny myself the urge to do emails and check Google News. My wife and kids are next, and because of that I quit running around with the "guys" years ago.

Having priorities in place creates a way to deny self those things that prevent us from being productive in our various roles and responsibilities.

The point I am trying to make is that until you've taken time to prioritize your life, you will never consistently achieve your goals. Developing priorities is the best way to deny self, and denying self is the best way to achieve goals.

One of the first business books I ever read was written by a sales guru named Tom Hopkins, and he had a slogan that he repeated to himself throughout every day; "I must do the most productive thing possible at every given moment." I modified this saying, based on my priorities, to "I must do the most productive thing possible at every given moment as a Christian soldier."

This all sounds difficult, but if you have your priorities in place, it is not hard to do. Idle chit chat, mindless Internet surfing, worthless television viewing and hanging out with negative faces in negative places all become things of the past.

I refer to my life today as a life where I am "running with a purpose," just like Paul shares with us in the scripture above.

Diving Deeper:

Additional Scripture: 1 Timothy 3:2-5, 2 Timothy 1:13-14, Matthew 6:33, Titus 1:5-9, Luke 6:45

Name IT: Are you running with a purpose these days?

Claim IT: If not, what is standing in your way?

Dump IT: Add the "what" from above to your Dump List and prayerfully turn it over to God one day at a time.

Effort

8-Handling setbacks and climbing mountains

Psalm 94: 17-19 (NIV), "Unless the Lord had given me help, I would soon have dwelt in the silence of death. When I said, 'My foot is slipping,' your love, O Lord, supported me. When anxiety was great within me, your consolation brought joy to my soul."

The longer I live, the more I realize that effectively handling setbacks is a real key in being able to consistently put forth productive effort.

Those of us who can view setbacks as nothing more than setups for future growth have the ability to get back up, wipe ourselves off, learn from the setback and continue to forge ahead. I know many people who have allowed setbacks to paralyze their dreams and goals for a lifetime, and it almost happened to me.

The biggest setback I've had to deal with in my life was the news that my second child was fighting for his life twelve hours after he was born "normal," and would subsequently be developmentally disabled his entire life. . .if he lived. I handled this setback like any good alcoholic/addict: I drank and drugged until it almost killed me. . .which was my second biggest setback.

As I look back on that period in my life, when I was losing everything I had worked so hard to get, and suicide seemed like the only answer, I am totally blown away when I think of where I am today; "I'm not worthy" is the phrase that comes to mind.

What got me through those major setbacks? Well, I'm glad you asked. It was God. As I was contemplating taking my life, I turned to God in a state of desperation and said the most powerful prayer known to man, "God, help me!"

Since that day, I've not let go of God. The Psalm above, written by David, fit my life on August 8, 1987, and it still holds true for me today.

Today I use God as a first, second, third, fourth, and fifth resort. I ask Him to guide me on my journey of achieving my dreams and goals, and then when a setback takes place I trust He allowed it to happen, I ask him for direction on how to handle the setback, and then I move on.

One thing we must never forget is the fact God is with us when we are on the top of mountains, and God is with us when we are in the muck of the creek bed in the valleys between the mountains.

The key is to stay tapped into His strength no matter what is happening, and the sooner we get up, wipe ourselves off, draw enlightenment from the setback, and begin climbing again, the sooner we are introduced to bigger and more beautiful mountains. In turn, we find ourselves on more of a continuous climb, where what used to be valleys are only dips in the path to the mountaintop.

The two biggest setbacks in my life have introduced me to "mountains" with opportunities and glorious views that I know are not humanly possible. I am grateful for those setbacks, but most of all I am grateful for an awesome God who helped me when *"I was about to settle for the silence of the grave."*

Remember, God is with you no matter where you are in your life. The key is asking Him for help early and often a day at a time.

Diving Deeper:

Additional Scripture: 1 Peter 2:19, 1 Peter 5:10-11, 2 Timothy 2:1-6

Name IT: Have you experienced setbacks in your life? How have you responded?

Claim IT: Is there one particular setback you've not been able to overcome?

Dump IT: Add the above setback to your Dump List and prayerfully turn it over to God one day at a time.

Attitude

8-A God-Righteous Attitude

Isaiah 32:17 (NIV), "The fruit of righteousness will be peace; the effect of righteousness will be quietness and confidence forever."

I can remember years ago, during a cell group meeting of Christian friends, we had a brief discussion on righteousness and self-righteousness. I shared with the group that the less self-righteous I become, the more I realize how much I don't know and in turn this creates a yearning for me to obtain "God-righteousness." The more I seek God-righteousness, the more righteous (right acting) I become.

Isaiah writes in chapter 32, verse 17: "And the effect of righteousness will be peace and the result of righteousness, quietness and trust forever."

Righteous is defined by Webster as: "acting in accord with divine or moral law." Today I yearn for righteousness, I yearn for the ability to act in accordance with God's laws and try real hard to stay away from "Jay's law." The reason for this is because I love peace. . .I am an ex-addict, and we addicts love peace! To be able to have peace among the severest of storms is something righteous living brings.

This is such a contrast to my self-righteous days. Self-righteous, as defined by Webster, is: "convinced of one's own righteousness." Self-righteousness entails having a closed mind and thinking, "it is my way or the highway." I can remember my mom calling me Mr. Know-It-All when I was growing up. I was so good at convincing myself that I was right and often tried to convince others. . .even when I was wrong.

Eventually I found that being convinced of my own righteousness was very dangerous for me, while on the other hand, having a yearning for God's righteousness is very peaceful for me.

It is amazing how my Christian walk has taken me farther and farther from being self-righteous and closer and closer to being righteous. I'm not there yet, and may never make it, but my life is so much more peaceful today as I try to live in accord with God's doctrine set forth for me in the Bible. The key to finding righteousness is to spend time in the Word and with others who know the Word.

Where are you with self-righteousness? If you often find yourself in arguments or in controversy over "right and wrong," try replacing the time spent in arguments with time in the Word or discussing the Word with another Jesus follower. Eventually "self" is replaced by God-righteousness, and turmoil is replaced by peace.

Diving Deeper:

Additional Scripture: Luke 6:27-29, 2 Corinthians 10:13-15, Galatians 6:3, Galatians 5:22-26, Proverbs 29:20

Name IT: Do you feel you are more God-righteous or self-righteous?

Claim IT: If you are self-righteous, why?

Dump IT: Add the "why" from above to your Dump List and prayerfully turn it over to God one day at a time.

Community

8-Lending to the Lord

Proverbs 19:17 (NIV), "He who is kind to the poor lends to the Lord, and he will reward him for what he has done."

There are hundreds of verses in the Bible pertaining to loving our neighbor and helping others. The Lord not only tells us to love and help others, but he "wired" us to be a blessing to others, otherwise we would all feel bad when we helped others. Does this make sense?

Think about this, have you ever had a "guilty conscience" when you've helped someone in need? I've never heard anyone who goes on mission trips, serves at soup kitchens, or gives clothing to the poor say they felt bad after doing it. I always hear them say how fulfilling it is to help others.

In the recovery community, our mental health is often dependent upon our willingness to get out of ourselves and help another person. All addictions, as well as most forms of mild to moderate depression, are selfish disorders born out of fear of something that has happened in our past.

When we are active in our disease, we very seldom take the time to get out of ourselves, and eventually the behavior insidiously becomes a habit and turns into a self-perpetuating cycle of self-focus and self-pity, causing us to become more of a burden than a blessing to the world. . .been there, done that.

I have a developmentally disabled son, and every morning when he gets on the bus, all of his comrades are upbeat, excited, saying hi, laughing, giggling. . .giving me my morning blessing of unconditional love. . .believe me, we are wired to give! My son and his buddies have not been warped by the world's "self-focused" point of view. Every time I put him on the bus, I am given a great gift by a bunch of people simply being the way God made them to be. They do not have a choice to be otherwise.

God does not lie, and what he says through Solomon in the Proverb above is very true. When you help the poor, you are helping the Lord, and even though true giving is performed without the need for repayment or reward, God repays us, and often it comes back ten-fold.

In Luke 6:38, Jesus says, "Give and you will receive. Your gift will return to you in full –pressed down, shaken together to make room for more, running over and poured into your lap. The amount you give will determine the amount you get back."

How do you spend the majority of your time today, giving or taking?

Diving Deeper:

Additional Scripture: Matthew 6:1-4, 2 Corinthians 8:2-7, Proverbs 21:13, Proverbs 29:7

Name IT: Do you try to help others whenever you can?

Claim IT: If not, then why?

Dump IT: Add the "why" from above to your Dump List and prayerfully turn it over to God one day at a time.

Energy

8-What are you "looking" like these days?

Proverbs 4:25 (NIV), "Let your eyes look straight ahead, fix your gaze directly before you."

Every now and then I travel to Las Vegas for business. I don't particularly like Vegas, but I try to make the most of it while I am there. One thing I do enjoy about Vegas is getting up at daybreak and running the Strip. I run for sixty minutes every day while I am there, and it is amazing what I see. Most of the people awake at that time of day are either running like me, or have yet been to bed from the previous night.

The ones who look as though they've not been to bed yet have a certain "look" on their faces. That "look" often falls into two categories: a look of "What did I just do?" and/or a look of "I've got to get a fix." The "look" is a very shallow, blank, desperate stare into space. I know about the "look" because I've seen pictures of myself back in my using days, and I had the "look," and although it is a look I am not proud of. The "look" reminds me of where I was and how far I've come.

Trouble is I see this "look" in more places than Vegas. The world and especially our country are at an all-time high of people with that "look." For some, this "look" has been brought on by the sudden loss of their job, for others it is brought on by being overextended in finances. I see the "look" on the faces of those who are cheating, lying, stealing, gossiping, and criticizing. I always see the "look" on the faces of those who are dependent upon other people, places, and things for happiness. The "look" is a "look" that is of the world and not of God. I found out a long time ago that happiness gained from the world is always temporary, it is never forever, and at some point the world lets us down.

It is so refreshing for me to get around true followers of Christ. They also have a "look." It is a look of peace, a look of freshness, a look of sureness. It is a deep look of faith. The look very seldom goes away, no matter what is going on in the world around them. The reason for the different "look" for Christ followers is that we've found what all of God's children are born looking for, and that is a relationship with God and the freedom from the bondage of sin that Christ's death and resurrection blesses us with.

But just because we've found God and accepted Jesus does not mean we can't lose it, and we lose it as soon as we start "looking" for our happiness from the world. That is why Solomon reminds us in the fourth Proverb to "fix our gaze directly before us."

One of the reasons I start my day in the Word and in prayer is to protect me from myself and my desire to be of the world before I am ever tempted. Prayer throughout the day also ensures that my eyes are looking straight ahead and not wandering into the world and when I am focused on the right things I have energy, an eternal type of energy.

Diving Deeper:

Additional Scripture: 1 John 5:4-5, 1 John 5:12, 1 John 2:15

Name IT: Do you waste time seeking joy from the world? Are you searching for peace from people, places, and things?

Claim IT: What are you seeking from the world
              that is getting in the way of becoming
              all God wants you to be?

Dump IT: Add the "what" from above to your
              Dump List and prayerfully turn it over
              to God one day at a time.

P.E.A.C.E.

CYCLE NINE OF TEN

Finding your purpose in life will not happen while doing nothing. Purpose is found somewhere along the path of doing something.

Plan

9-"Bound" to continue...

Proverbs 25:28 (NIV), "Like a city whose walls are broken down is a man who lacks self-control."

*H*as the following scenario ever happened to you You make a decision to change, you pray about it, God actually starts intervening on your behalf through other people, places, and things, but you are unable to control your urges to go back to your old ways? You begin "constructing new walls to your city," as Solomon talks about in Proverbs 25, and then the walls begin to weaken, and eventually they come crumbling down. . .again.

One of the keys in keeping our walls strong and in place is to develop self-control, and self-control only happens for me if I have a **PLAN**. My past of virtually destroying and losing everything serves as a great reminder to me how much self-control I have. My self-control is totally dependent upon having and working a plan.

Plans give us **boundaries,** they allow us to keep our priorities straight, and give us the ability to say no to outside forces that try to pull us away from the plan.

The planning process initially requires the willingness to commit an hour or two, and sometimes more, to prioritizing what needs to happen, envisioning what you want to happen, and then reducing it to writing, i.e., transforming the dreams into goals.

For example, maybe your number one goal for this year is to become a better spouse. If this is the case, then you need to take time to envision what this looks like and reduce this picture to writing. There is something "magical" about writing things down. For me, writing somehow indelibly etches the goal in my brain, and the more I write, the better my chances become of achieving my goals.

The next step to effective planning is to commit an hour every Sunday towards creating a day-by-day plan for the following week. Planning the days in hourly increments is the most effective way to stay "bound" to the plan. I find this hour on Sunday also helps me better prepare for everything I have going on in my life throughout the week. It prevents me from over-committing and/or under-committing. It keeps me on time and on task during the week.

Next, the planning process involves the daily ritual of reviewing the plan for the new day, in the morning (preferably after morning prayer, and devotions. . .during which the plan is committed to the Lord. . .see Proverbs 16:3 and Mark 11:24).

Finally, as the day is about to close, it is important to take a few minutes to take an inventory of the day and make any needed adjustments to the plan for tomorrow.

The final step also involves prayer, where we thank God for His help with our plan for that day, and seek His help and guidance for tomorrow's plan.

I love the quote by Lewis Carroll, "If you don't know where you're going, any road will take you there."

Make a decision today to decide where you want to go by developing a plan. Make a decision to "continue to continue" by planning weekly and daily. If you do this, you are "bound" to see major improvements in your life.

Diving Deeper:

Additional Scripture: Proverbs 16:3, Mark 11:24, James 1:12

Name IT: Do you have a plan you are working?

Claim IT: If not, why?

Dump IT: Add the "why" from above to your Dump List and prayerfully turn it over to God one day at a time.

Effort

9- Work Smart

Proverbs 13:4 (NIV), "The sluggard craves and gets nothing, but the desires of the diligent are fully satisfied."

As I pointed out previously, putting forth productive effort takes more than **hard work.** In fact, if we don't avoid time-wasters like excessive talk, excuses, setback paralysis, and thinking we have all the answers, our **work** becomes **hard** and it becomes harder and harder to **work hard**. . .confused yet?

In other words, if we don't learn how to **work smart,** we will never be able to reap the benefits of hard work, which is paramount in generating productive effort and in-turn generating productive results.

I'm sure you've all witnessed someone who works endlessly but never gets anything done. People who "work" like this become no more productive than the "sluggard" Solomon refers to in Proverb 13. The word "diligent" is used to counter "sluggard" in the Proverb above, and diligent as defined in Webster's means, "steady, earnest, and energetic application and effort." It means working smart *and* working hard.

The legendary basketball coach, John Wooden, once said: "The harder I work, the luckier I get." I've read some of Coach Wooden's books and he was the best at working efficiently and diligently. He was the best at working smart and this enabled him to work even harder. The results of his work in college basketball will most likely never be eclipsed. He is the greatest of all time. (Whether you like basketball or not, I suggest you read Wooden's book, "Wooden On Leadership.")

We've all heard the cliché's, "Practice makes perfect," "You get what you work for," "No pain, no gain." Working hard is the key ingredient in creating productive effort. Combining working smart with working hard is the absolute formula for consistently generating diligent work effort and productive results.

I became a pretty good basketball player because I was diligent in practicing daily. I am a pretty effective husband and dad because I work at it every day.

I got sober and stayed sober not only because of the love and grace of God, but because of the work I put forth in staying sober. Back in late 1987, during my first ninety days of sobriety, I attended 120 AA (Alcoholics Anonymous) meetings and went to forty counseling sessions. . .amazing what a life and death proposition does to your work ethic.

Putting forth productive effort is a process and not an event. The best way to see whether or not you are working diligently is to measure how smart and hard you are working.

Keep a log for a couple of weeks and document the time you spend in "time-wasters," like nonsensical talk, web surfing, face booking, TV watching, etc.. . . Write down every time you verbalize an excuse or tell yourself you just can't do it. Then keep track of how much time you spend learning and being teachable, and how much time you are "working" at whatever your goal is.

Eliminating time-wasters, excuses, and procrastination, while growing an attitude of teach-ability and a creating a willingness to work smart, will not only generate productive effort and positive results, but lots and lots of luck!

Diving Deeper:

Additional Scripture: Titus 3:14, Proverbs 28:19, Proverbs 21:5,

Name IT: Do you use your time effectively? Do you struggle with time-wasters? Do you practice to become better?

Claim IT: What time-wasters do you struggle with the most?

Dump IT: Add the time wasters from above to your Dump List and prayerfully turn them over to God one day at a time.

Attitude

9-Beliefs and Attitudes

Jeremiah 29:11-14 (NIV), "For I know the plans I have for you," says the Lord, "plans to prosper you and not to harm you, plans to give you hope and a future. Then you will call upon me and come and pray to me, and I will listen to you. You will seek me and find me when you seek me with all your heart. I will be found by you,"

In my years of helping others, I have found that a person's beliefs will eventually make or break them. From our beliefs we have thoughts, and from our thoughts we take action and from our actions we create results. The results, most of the time, coincide with our beliefs. If we believe we are going to succeed, we will eventually succeed. If we believe we will fail, we will fail.

Our beliefs are developed over the years from life experiences. Most of them date back to when we were quite young. What is so sad for me to handle is when a lie becomes a belief, and in turn that lie prevents people from being everything God wants them to be. As God tells us in Jeremiah, he has great plans for us, but sometimes the world and other people try to convince us otherwise.

I can remember sitting in a Twelve Step meeting years ago when a young man in his twenties said he finally figured out why he was a piece of "crap" (edited for this devotional); it was because his dad told him he was a piece of "crap" early and often every day throughout his childhood, teen, and early adult years. The good news for this man is that he recognized it and was ready to overcome this paralyzing belief of worthlessness his dad had bestowed upon him.

Will power is often not enough to change destructive and paralyzing beliefs, especially when these beliefs have been a part of us for much of our lives. Many people know the above verse from Jeremiah 29:11 but fail to read and act upon the three verses after it. God does indeed want us to have a prosperous future, and He tells us how to obtain it in verses 12-14: *"Then you will call upon me and come and pray to me, and I will listen to you. You will seek me and find me when you seek me with all your heart. I will be found by you. . ."*

God gives us three steps to follow:

1. **Call** Him and come and pray to Him and He will listen. (i.e., pray, pray, pray)

2. **Seek** Him with all our heart and we will find Him. (i.e., ALL means ALL. . .our toxic beliefs spread like cancer to ALL aspects of our life, and for God to eradicate them we must surrender ALL to Him, or He cannot fix us.)

3. **Find** Him. (This is often the most difficult part, as we expect God to show up with the answer in person, and unless you are Moses, it doesn't happen that way. God usually shows up in the form of other people, scripture, and/or the books we are reading. Thus the reason to hang around people who have beliefs you want, read the Bible daily, and read books about the beliefs you are trying to attain.)

If you are paralyzed by beliefs that are nothing but lies told to you from the past, start calling, seeking, and finding the Lord, and He will indeed prosper you.

Diving Deeper:

Additional Scripture: 2 Peter 2:19, 1 John 3:18-20, Ephesians 6:10-18

Name IT: Are you paralyzed by lies that have become beliefs?

Claim IT: What actions result from the beliefs that you know are probably lies?

Dump IT: Add any and all beliefs that you know are lies to your Dump List and prayerfully turn them over to God one day at a time.

Community

9-A Gift We All Have

1 John 4:16 (NIV), "God is love. Whoever lives in love lives in God and God in him."

Recently I was talking with my wife, and she was marveling at how many people know our developmentally disabled son. Our son cannot talk, he still wears a diaper, and pretty much requires total care. He has gone to school and some type of special program for most of his life and along the way he has obviously made many friends, and he hasn't said a word.

He has a smile that is magnetic. He does not know hate. He often goes up to strangers, gives them a smile, grabs their hand, and goes for a walk. He totally trusts everyone, he doesn't care what the color of a person's skin is, and it makes no difference what sins one may have committed. He couldn't care less about the type of car you drive, the house you live in, or how much money you make. If he smiles at you and you smile at him, he has just created another friend.

How simple yet full our lives could be if we didn't allow our brains to cause us to complicate things. Being kind and loving to our fellow man is not something we learn or earn or pay for. It is something that is born into each and every one of us. Try not talking, judging, and comparing for a day, and you will get a feel for how my son feels every day of his life. . .this is the way God created us to be.

My son has taught me that this life is not about making, taking, complaining, or consuming. This life is about giving love to one another. This is a gift we are all born with, and my son is living proof of that.

Thank you, Jordan!

Diving Deeper:

Additional Scripture: Mark 11:25, Luke 10:38-42, 1 John 4:7-21

Name IT: Do you know someone like my son? Does he or she exude love and acceptance whenever you are around them? How does it make you feel?

Claim IT: Do you believe God wires us to be forgiving, accepting, and all-loving? If so, do you live this way?

Dump IT: Note on your Dump List anything that is preventing you from loving the way God wired you to love and prayerfully turn it over to God one day at a time.

Energy

9-The MAIN THING

Isaiah 40:31 (NIV), "But those who trust in the Lord will find new strength. They will soar high on wings like eagles. They will run and not grow weary. They will walk and not faint."

A few years ago, I read the book, "How the Mighty Fail," by Jim Collins.

In "How the Mighty Fail," Collins researches and details the reasons why companies that were one time considered successful, end up failing. He does a great job of describing the stages these once-great companies experienced prior to their ultimate demise and death. The bottom line is all of these companies did not keep the "main thing the main thing." They forgot what got them to their level of greatness, they took their eye off the ball, became arrogant, and by the time they figured out they were failing, it was too late.

In my years as a businessman, I constantly reminded myself and the leaders of our business what the "main things" were. In any business, the "main things" are the customers, the employees, and the shareholders. If you don't try your best to listen to and take care of these critical components of your business, it will eventually fail.

Keeping the main thing the main thing is critical to the success of anything, whether it be marriage, parenting, work, finances, recovery, or most importantly our Christian walk.

Keeping the main thing the main thing as a Christian means asking God to drive all aspects of our lives including our work, business, relationships, parenting, finances, and recovery. This happens when every day is started in prayer and in the Word, and this simple act allows us to die to ourselves, and in turn allows God to live through us and ultimately run the show.

We've all heard this simple yet powerful prayer: "I can't, God can, I think I'll let him." I've been doing this little prayer ritual (the first three steps of the Twelve Steps) in various forms every morning since I got sober in 1987. The results have been nothing less than amazing, and the only credit I give to myself is having the willingness to keep the MAIN THING the MAIN THING, right out of the gate each and every day; the rest of the credit goes to the Lord.

It always amazes me how much energy I receive after going through my morning devotions.

Are you keeping the MAIN THING the MAIN THING these days?

Diving Deeper:

Additional Scripture: Psalm 119:1-5, Psalm 121:1-8, Hebrews 4:12-13

Name IT: Are you keeping the main thing the main thing?

Claim IT: If not, what is preventing you from keeping the main thing the main thing?

Dump IT: Add the "what" from above to your Dump List and prayerfully turn it over to God one day at a time.

P.E.A.C.E.

CYCLE TEN OF TEN

The depth of your life is proportionate to the depth of your faith. Your faith will never grow deep by living your life in the shallow end.

Plan

10-Plan for Obedience

Proverbs 21:3 (NIV), "To do what is right and just is more acceptable to the Lord than sacrifice."

I remember a few years ago, when I caught up with a friend who is in recovery. He had sought help from me for his problem, and I turned him onto a sober living place that has transformed the lives of many men over the years.

Upon his entrance into this sober living place, my friend had nothing, as his various addictions had taken everything, including his reputation and pride. Today he is transformed, and it all happened because of his willingness to seek out help from others who knew the way, and his willingness to accept Jesus as his Lord and savior on a daily basis.

When I met up with my friend, I asked him if the place where he got transformed offered the Twelve Steps (as you know, I am a big supporter of The Twelve Steps). He said, "No, the entire foundation of this transformational program was based on understanding the freedom obtained through Jesus' death for our sin and the willingness to accept the power of the Holy Spirit in order to try our best to live right and not sin." He went on to say, "We were taught to seek God's power on a daily basis to do right and in turn be blessed." I totally agreed with him and shared with him what my pastor often says: "God blesses obedience."

Over the years, I have found there is more than one way to find and experience the transforming powers of Jesus Christ and subsequent blessings, but the key to experiencing the fruits of this transformational relationship on a daily basis is just as my friend said: "Doing right."

Sober and serene living is about doing right and being obedient to God's will. This is not an easy task for those of us who've created habitual behavior that is wrong, and most of this "wrong" behavior is destructive behavior towards ourselves.

The key to doing right is to first figure out what is wrong and look at the consequences created by wrong behavior. Then take a look at your right behavior and the blessings it creates.

Keep in mind, in the early transformational stages, most of us are unable to determine right from wrong and need counselors, sponsors, mentors support groups. . .and of course God (through prayer) to help set us straight.

After figuring out what right is, we need to work on putting to death, on a daily basis, our wrong behavior and replace it with right behavior. It takes some time to break a habit, and the first three or four weeks of replacing wrong with right is not easy, but it is the only way it will happen.

If you are struggling with continuous, habitual, wrong behavior, start over today. Create a plan of obedience. Write on a piece of paper what right-living is to you and ask God for His help in helping you live in His righteousness.

A plan of obedience is a plan that will be blessed. . .I write from experience.

Diving Deeper:

Additional Scripture: Matthew 25:31-46, Colossians 3:5, Revelation 22:11-12

Name IT: Do you know the difference between right and wrong behavior?

Claim IT: Reflect and think back to the blessings you've missed or problems you've created from wrong behavior.

Dump IT: Place any wrong behavior you still struggle with on your Dump List and prayerfully turn them over to God one day at a time. (Since this is the beginning of cycle ten I am assuming your list already contains this behavior.)

Effort

10-The Eternal Boss

Ephesians 6:5-8 (NIV), "Slaves obey your earthly masters with respect and fear, and with sincerity of heart, just as you would obey Christ. Obey them not only to win their favor when their eye is on you, but like slaves of Christ, doing the will of God from your heart. Serve wholeheartedly, as if you were serving the Lord, not men, because you know that the Lord will reward everyone for whatever good he does, whether he is slave or free."

As noted previously, productive effort not only involves working hard and smart, but we need to make sure we use our time effectively, avoid excuses, learn from our setbacks, and remain teachable.

I know people who do all of the above, but are stuck in a work situation or are working for an organization or playing on a team where putting forth productive effort doesn't seem to matter. No matter how hard they try or how productive they are, they never seem fulfilled because whatever they do is never enough.

In Ephesians chapter 6 above, Paul reminds us that our effort should never be dependent upon who we are working for in the flesh, because no matter what we do, we are to serve wholeheartedly as if we are working for the Lord.

Something else to consider is the fact that God owns everything, and at the end of the day we are always working for Him.

"To the Lord your God belong the heavens, even the highest heavens, the earth and everything in it." (Deuteronomy 10:14, NIV)

Therefore, we should always put forth our best effort no matter who we are working for, that is, if we are walking the Christian walk. What is even cooler is the fact we will be rewarded for doing this. . ."**the Lord will reward everyone for whatever good he does whether he is slave or free."**

Once we understand *who* we are working for, the final step in putting forth productive effort is to seek God's guidance and direction with our work. If we do this, no matter how difficult the task or the taskmaster, we will be rewarded and always succeed because God is one boss who always wants us to succeed.

I've sought God's direction and help since 1987 with my business career, and it has been nothing less than amazing because I had a Boss who wanted me to win.

Work hard, work smart, avoid time-wasters, avoid excuses, know there will be setbacks, and always remain teachable, but most importantly, never forget who the Boss is and you will be blown away by the results of your effort.

Diving Deeper:

Additional Scripture: Philippians 2:12-16, 1 Corinthians 3:9, Ephesians 2:10

Name IT: When you work, do you always put forth your best effort, regardless of who the boss is? Do you work as if you are working for God?

Claim IT: Note some times in your life you have put in less than your best effort. Why did you not give your best effort?

Dump IT: Add to your Dump List anything that is standing in your way of working as if you were working for God. Prayerfully turn this over to God one day at a time.

Attitude

10-"Day-mares" and Attitude

Philippians 4:6-7 (NIV), "Do not be anxious about anything, but in everything, by prayer and petition, with thanksgiving, present your requests to God. And the peace of God, which transcends all understanding, will guard your hearts and your minds in Christ Jesus."

A favorite "quick read" of mine is "The Four Agreements," by Don Miguel Ruiz. In "The Four Agreements" Ruiz focuses on the four key elements in creating freedom, peace, and happiness in life.

1. Be impeccable with your word
2. Never make assumptions
3. Don't take things personally
4. Always give your best effort

A key to recovery is taking ongoing personal inventories. During my "spot-check" inventories, I often review these four areas outlined in Ruiz's book, and reflect on how well I managed them.

All of us have a weakness in one or more of these areas, but in my years of helping people with addiction and co-dependency problems, the "biggie" is **taking things personally,** and second in line is **making assumptions,** and when the two are combined a state of mind that I refer to as a "day-mare" most likely will occur.

A day-mare is an illogical state of mind that occurs while awake, and is a result of combining super sensitivity with incorrect assumptions. For example: "He or she didn't say hi to me, so therefore he or she must not like me." Or how about this one: "I can't believe Suzy didn't thank me for the gift I got her for her graduation, she must not have liked the gift." Or, "My boss told me I needed to improve my performance, therefore my boss doesn't like me and I bet one of my co-workers complained to my boss about me."

I will never forget the time I once "thought" I got snubbed in church by someone because when I attempted to shake his hand, he abruptly turned away from me. I "assumed" he was "blowing me off," and it hurt my super-sensitive, self-absorbed personality. This situation did not turn into a full-blown day-mare for me because I used some tools to minimize it, but every time I saw this person I wondered what I did to tick him off. Then about six months after the "snub," I found out this person had minimal vision and was blind. The poor guy didn't even see me and I just assumed he didn't like me. Can you say super-sensitive?

What a fool I was, and can still be if I assume and take things personally. The committee in my head (Satan's committee) loves to create chaos and day-mares, and although it happens a lot less now than it used to, I can almost count on it happening when I am self-absorbed and isolated.

Preventing day-mares is pretty simple. . .don't assume and don't take things personally. Whenever you begin thinking someone is out to get you or doesn't like you. . . .99 percent of the time you are incorrect because you simply are not that important.

Another tool to use when the "committee" starts stirring things up is to pray the simple "by the blood of Jesus, Satan/day-mares be gone" prayer. If that doesn't work, call your accountability partner and LISTEN. Another great way to get out of day-mares is to get out of self and help someone in need.

Life is too short to be super-sensitive. Learn how to laugh at yourself. I still laugh at myself today when I think about the time that poor man with impaired vision "offended" me. This is proof to me that I am but one incorrect "assumption" away from creating a day-mare. How about you?

Diving Deeper:

Additional Scripture: James 4:1-2, 1 Corinthians 13:4-7, 2 Timothy 3:2-3

Name IT: Are you super-sensitive? Do you take everything too personally? Do you find yourself making assumptions without facts and in turn creating "day-mares"?

Claim IT: What causes this sensitivity? Why do you assume?

Dump IT: Add the "what" and "why" from above to your Dump List and prayerfully turn them over to God one day at a time.

Community

10-No Eggs and Community Time

Philippians 4:11-12 (NIV), "I am not saying this because I am in need, for I have learned to be content whatever the circumstances. I know what it is to be in need, and I know what it is to have plenty. I have learned the secret of being content in any and every situation, whether well fed or hungry, whether living in plenty or in want.

As far as I can remember, I've always had to have eggs for breakfast, and if meat and potatoes were thrown in, I had what I considered a great breakfast. I believe this is just a part of my German heritage.

I remember a time when we were on a family vacation and we were staying at a hotel owned by my favorite chain. I'd been staying at this particular brand of hotels ever since I started traveling in business many years previous. The reason I always chose this particular chain is because. . .you guessed it. . .they serve eggs with their free breakfast. But on the first morning of this particular stay there were no eggs. I was distraught and quickly told my wife I was heading out to find a place that had eggs and I would be back shortly.

It did not take me long to find a restaurant that served breakfast, and as I was standing in line I noticed the gentleman in front of me asked for a cup of ice water. When the waitress asked if he needed to be seated, he told her, "No, I am homeless, and all I want is a cup of ice water." He was given the ice water and he turned to head out the door. I looked at him and said, "Hey, come with me, it looks as though you could use some breakfast." You would have thought I had handed him a million dollars as his eyes lit up and he followed me to our booth.

Over my years of working with and helping others, I have a couple of questions I always ask that help me figure out what is going on in someone's life pretty quickly. One of the first questions I always ask is whether or not they believe in God. When I asked my new friend this question, he proceeded to tell me he was not into organized religion but he believed in Jesus and his teachings.

Then I asked him why he was homeless, and he proceeded to tell me that he had arrived in Fort Collins in hopes of having work to do, and things didn't work out as planned. He had run out of money, had no work, and had spent the last ten days sleeping behind and eating out of dumpsters while trying to find a way back home to Tampa.

He shared with me that he had stopped by at least a half-dozen churches, and each one of them told him they could not help him. After hearing all of this, I asked him if he was angry at God because the churches had not come through for him. He looked at me and said, "No." Then he saw I had my Bible with me (I was planning on doing my morning devotions while eating breakfast), and he asked me if he could look at it.

He quickly leafed through some pages and turned to the passage above in Philippians and read it to me. He proceeded to tell me that if he was really walking the Christian walk, it meant that he had to be content **WHATEVER** the circumstance. He also said that he has been praying without ceasing and trusted that God would take care of him during this most difficult time. But then he also said to me that he was getting dazed and confused because he kept running into dead ends, but continued to believe "he could do everything through Jesus who gives him his strength." His knowledge of the Bible totally blew me away.

This of course opened the door for me to talk openly about my faith, and we talked for a good forty-five minutes. When the waitress came to give me the bill, she told me the restaurant would pay for my friend's portion of the bill and they also filled up a box of food for him.

As we were getting ready to leave, he thanked me for taking the time to feed him and talk with him. I told him that he had given me so much more than I had given him, and I told him to jump in my car and I would take him to the bus station and get him a bus ticket to go home to Tampa. . .he was blown away.

My journal entry for Tuesday, July 20th, 2010 has no scripture or personal reflection noted. The only thing I wrote down for that day was my friend's name and "No Eggs." I am so grateful my hotel did not have eggs that morning, because it allowed me to have my faith strengthened and renewed by someone who had absolutely nothing but faith and a content heart. I am grateful for God giving me the willingness to be aware of and to help those in the community around me on that morning. Otherwise, I would have missed out on a huge blessing.

P.S. After explaining to the family what had happened, when I arrived back to the hotel an hour later than promised, my father-in-law laughed and told me it had to have been a God thing, because five minutes after I left the hotel, they brought out a big pan of scrambled eggs.

Diving Deeper:

Additional Scripture: Psalm 36:16-17, Proverbs 17:1, Proverbs 22:2, James 2:6, Galatians 2:9-10

Name IT: Do you help the poor when presented with the opportunity? Why or why not?

Claim IT: What prevents you from helping people in need?

Dump IT: Add the "what" from above to your Dump List and prayerfully turn it over to God one day at a time.

Energy

10-Spiritual Progress

2 Peter 1:5-8 (NIV), "For this very reason, make every effort to add to your faith, goodness, and to goodness, knowledge, and to knowledge, self-control; and to self-control, perseverance, and to persever-

ance, godliness; and to godliness, brotherly kindness; and to brotherly kindness, love. For if you possess these qualities to increasing measure, they will keep you from being ineffective and unproductive in your knowledge of our Lord Jesus Christ."

"You can strive for perfection, your goal can be perfection, your focus can be on perfection but if you **require** perfection in anything you do in life. . .you will never be happy." Gino Auriemma, University of Connecticut women's basketball coach. . .as his team was closing in on a perfect season back in 2009.

At the beginning of most Alcoholics Anonymous (AA) meetings the beginning of Chapter 5 (How it Works), from the "Big Book of Alcoholics Anonymous," is read. "How it Works" explains the twelve spiritual steps of AA and the role they play in giving the hopeless, hope. The first time I heard, "How it Works," there was one part that really jumped out at me. . ."*Many of us exclaimed, 'What an order! I can't go through with it.' Do not be discouraged. No one among us has been* *able to maintain anything like perfect adherence to these principles. We are not saints. The point is that we are willing to grow along spiritual lines. The principles we have set down are guides to progress. **We claim spiritual progress rather than spiritual perfection.***"

Considering where I was in my life, spiritual progress made me feel like I had a chance at "getting" this God thing that many people in recovery told me was my only hope for continuous sobriety. For years I thought I had to have it all together to receive God's grace, but spiritual progress gave me a new perspective on things. As I've grown in my faith over the years, I totally understand why God had his son serve as the sacrificial lamb for all of our mess ups. He gives us no excuse for ever giving up on our spiritual journey. It is through Christ's death that we've been given new life.

Over the years, as I have grown closer to Jesus, I find myself desiring to get even closer. This desire to grow closer to Jesus is because of a new, healthy addiction I have to the fruits of the Spirit. Where I once thought the fruits of the spirit (love, joy, peace, patience, kindness, goodness, faithfulness, gentleness and self-control. . .Galatians 5:22) were reserved for only the perfect, I find myself experiencing them more days than not. Do you believe in miracles?

This post came to me as I was reading the scripture above. Simon Peter was talking about the process involved in attaining the "fruits." He was telling us that attaining the "fruits" is a step-by-step process that eventually gives us the energy to be effective and productive for the Lord Jesus Christ, which simply means bringing others to Him.

If you are a Christian and struggling right now, take a moment and reflect on your journey. Have you made progress? If you have, then you're on the right path. This whole spiritual journey is definitely a process, not an event. If you seem to be having trouble making progress, try working a Twelve Step Program. The Twelve Steps are a great way to ensure you are progressing on your spiritual journey. After all, that is "How it Works."

Diving Deeper:

Additional Scripture: Isaiah 40:31, 2 Samuel 22:31, 2 Corinthians 5:17, 2 Corinthians 3:12, Romans 5:1-5

Name IT: Do you view your faith life as a journey? If you do, is the journey moving forward, standing still, or going backwards?

Claim IT: Are there times you find your journey is not going the way you want it to go? Do you think you have to be perfect to please God?

Dump IT: Add the one thing that continues to get in your way of progressing on your spiritual journey to your Dump List. I am thinking/hoping by now. . .50 days into this process. . .you have nothing to add. If you do, prayerfully turn it over to God one day at a time.

This is a Beginning, not an End. . .

◯

*C*ongratulations, you've just completed the most important fifty-day journey of your life!

Over the past fifty days, you have been asked to take an honest look at your defects and shortcomings and "Dump" them, on a daily basis. For best results, continue to turn your "Dumps" over to God on a daily basis until they are no longer an obstacle.

You've also studied over 150 scripture verses all breathed by God. How cool is that?

This "50-Day Life Transforming Journey" has now turned into a daily habit of: reflection, scripture reading, dumping, and prayer which will in-turn pump your life to new heights.

Get ready for the ride of your life. . .I write from experience.

P.E.A.C.E.

Dump List

<u>Dump List</u>

Dump List

Dump List

CPSIA information can be obtained at www.ICGtesting.com
Printed in the USA
BVOW08s1513190713

326349BV00003B/4/P